CREATIVE ECONOMICS

CREATIVE ECONOMICS

*YOUR GUIDE TO CREATIVE
OPPORTUNITIES*

DONNA MCNEILL

To order additional copies of this book, contact:
Xlibris LLC
1-888-795-4274
www.Xlibris.com
Orders@Xlibris.com
553261

CONTENTS

PREFACE

I don't know about you, but the job market sucks. Many companies are not hiring, especially if you have been unemployed for a length of time. So what can you do? Do you just throw your hands up in the air and give up? Creative Economics is a book created with you in mind. If you have been out of the job market a long time, laid off or fired, wanting to work for yourself, or just a second income, this book is going to revolutionize how you think about seeking employment opportunities. Let's face it; it is a struggle to go from one job interview to another trying to convince someone that you are the right candidate for the job. Creative Economics brings fresh, bold and unique opportunities that allow you to create your own niche, and not be in an over-saturated career field doing what everyone else in that field is doing.

Join the Revolution!

BUSINESS START-UP

So you want to start a business and you may not know where to begin. Before you can even plunge into the idea of a business, it is a good idea to know the things that are required to start one. The following steps will give you guidance as to what you need to do to get started.

1. Creating an Effective Business and Marketing Plan for Your Business.
2. Deciding on a Business Name.
3. Registering Your Name at Your Local County Clerk's Office.
4. Deciding What Type of Entity Do You Want Your Business to Be.
5. Filing the Necessary Paperwork to Define Your Business.
6. Tax ID Number and Bank Account.
7. Intellectual Property and Copyrights.
8. Finding Financing for Your Business Venture.
9. Placing an Ad in the Paper to Advertise Your Business Start-Up.
10. Establishing Your Office Space.
11. Setting up Your Filing System.
12. Setting up Your Accounting System.
13. Ordering or Printing Your Stationery and Other Business Advertisements.
14. Establishing a Website for Your Business.

This may seem like a lot to do, but this is the process you need to follow in order to establish a business. When you establish a business initially, you should maintain some type of steady income. For example, you shouldn't quit your job anticipating that you will be making very good money overnight. It is easier to start out part-time, and maintain your full-time or part-time job to make ends meet until your business is successful. It may take several years, before you turnover a profit.

1. *Creating an Effective Business and Marketing Plan for Your Business.*

This is the entree for any type of business that you may consider. For example, your business plan is what you will present to potential lending institutions, banks, investors, small business associations. These projections will tell your potential investors what you forecast your profits to be for your business. These financial institutions, investors, government agency, and banks, will evaluate your business plan and/or marketing plan to determine if your idea or business will be worthy of lending you funds to help start-up your business. You should also look into various courses and resources that will help you locate funding. You don't have to rely on just one resource, and you should know the ins and outs of what is expected of your investor(s). Sometimes, you may find a private investor who is only interested in investing in your business, whereas you may find some who want some type of control or say in the business decisions.

2. *Deciding on a Business Name.*

3. *Registering Your Name at Your Local County Clerk's Office*

You will have to determine a business name for your business venture and it cannot be a name that is already being used by a business in the area (or county) where you will be doing business. Your county clerk's office will have a list of businesses names, which are names that are taken, and you will have to determine if the name that you want is not already used by another local business. It would be a good idea to come up with several names in the event that one of the names is taken. There are documents that you will have to fill out to establish your name, and once it has been established, no one else can use that particular name. There are fees associated with name registration, which you will have to contact your local county clerk's office to determine how much it will cost.

4. Deciding What Type of Entity Do You Want Your Business to Be

In addition to deciding on a business name, you will have to establish whether you want to have a sole proprietorship, Limited Liability Company, partnership, or a corporation. A sole proprietorship is the simplest structure, and it is usually run by one individual who owns and operates the business (19).

A partnership is operated by several individuals. Partnerships can be either general or limited. In a general partnership, the partners manage the company and assume responsibility for the partnership's debts and other obligations. In the limited partnership, the general partners own and operate the business, while the limited partners are considered investors only.

With a corporation, the business becomes an independent legal entity, separate from its owners, and as such, it requires complying with more regulations and tax requirements. For small business owners, the S Corporation is more attractive than the C Corporation. With an S Corporation, income and losses are passed through to shareholders and included on their individual tax returns. This results in only one level of federal tax to pay.

Limited Liability Company is considered a hybrid of partnerships and corporations, taking the best features of both. LLC's enjoy the protection of corporations, without the double taxation of standard corporations.

Nonprofit Corporation are eligible for certain benefits, such as income tax exemptions, sales and property exemptions.

5. Filing the Necessary Paperwork to Define Your Business

It is important to file all necessary paperwork, such as obtaining a business license and/or permits. Also, it would be a good idea to consult with a lawyer to find out, based on the type of business you plan on conducting, what type of license or permit is necessary. For example, is it necessary to obtain health department permits, liquor licenses, fire department permits, air and water pollution control permits, sign permit, county permits, state licenses, or federal license?

6. *Tax ID Number and Bank Account*

It would be a good idea to obtain a separate bank account in your business name, and also a Tax ID number. You will have to contact the Internal Revenue Service in order to get the appropriate paperwork to apply for a tax ID number, or if you can afford an accountant and/or lawyer, they will be able to file the necessary paperwork.

7. *Intellectual Property and Copyrights.*

If your idea is an original invention or an improvement of a current idea, you will want to know about intellectual property and patents. For anything that is originally written, photographed, recorded, etc., you will want to find out about copyrights to protect your investment or idea. It is worth making the effort to protect your idea. Although copyright laws have loosened up over the years, stating that any work that has been written is protected without you having to file a formal copyright application, you should file the application to have it on record that you have in fact authored a particular work or created an invention.

8. *Finding Financing for Your Business Venture.*

You will definitely need some type of financial support unless you have savings on your own. The best way to start is with family and friends. If these resources aren't enough, there are many government agencies that will help to fund your business venture. One particular agency is the Small Business Administration (SBA). They offer various workshops to help you with business basics. Some of the equipment that you may need to run your business can be financed without credit. For example, on some TV infomercials and websites for various items, companies will allow you to set up a payment plan in order to try the item for a period of time, and you can return it if you are not satisfied. If you plan to keep the item, they will bill your credit card monthly for the balance owed.

9. *Placing an Ad in the Paper to Advertise Your Business*

Start-Up

In some states, you may be required to place an ad in the paper in order to advertise that you have started a business. You will have to check with your state to determine the necessary steps, or if this is a necessary requirement.

10. *Establishing Your Office Space*

If you have the space or corner in your home, this may be the cheapest way to establish your office space. If space and family traffic is an issue, you may want to look in the newspaper or on the Internet to find office space. There are some advertisements for office space where you can rent an office within a business. There are other places that allow you to rent space based on the number of hours, where sometimes, you will be able to share the office equipment within the building.

11. *Setting up Your Filing System.*

If necessary, you will need to establish a filing system to keep all documents organized. For example, you may want to have a business start-up file, client files, vendor files, etc. Keeping things filed and organized is a great way to save time looking for things or paperwork getting lost. An electronic filing system is ideal for individuals who want to be green. This cuts down on the clutter. In any event, be able to lock your drawers to maintain the privacy of your company and your clients.

12. *Setting up Your Accounting System*

An investment in a good accounting/bookkeeping system is ideal in maintaining accurate books for potential/current investors, banks, tax purposes and accounting purposes. Maintaining good books allows you to establish, which parts of your business are profitable and which are actually losing money. If you are doing your own bookkeeping, you can have a professional accountant evaluate your business to help review the accuracy of your books and to correct any financial problems that may arise in your books.

13. *Having Your Stationery and Other Business Advertisements*

Now that you have gone through all the steps to ensure that you business is financially able and established, you will want to have professional stationary to market your business. Having professional stationary is a must in communicating with other businesses, such as potential clients, investors, vendors, etc. A good start is professional envelopes and letterhead, with professional business cards. Being able to network is essential, and handing someone your business card will allow you to connect with individuals who can help you with your business or become potential clients. Having a nice portfolio, depending on your business, with samples of your work is a great marketing tool.

14. *Establishing a Website for Your Business.*

With the evolution of the Internet, a website is almost mandatory in advertising your business to give it a global presence. A website allows you to easily connect with consumers outside of your local area without advertising locally. Always keep in mind that every business doesn't require a website, so you will have to use your discretion to determine if you can service a market outside of your local area. Websites cannot hurt your business, but if you are unable to create your own website and want to consult a professional to build your website to meet your needs, you will have to assess whether you are able to afford one, as well as whether it is necessary.

Although there are many steps that you will follow in starting up your small business, the rewards are worth the effort. You will have to decide if you have the endurance to weather the storms, because this book is not written to deceive you and make you believe that you will be an overnight success or a millionaire. I hope that this book will give you ideas in establishing your own business, and revolutionize the way you think about looking for income opportunities. I hope this book will bring much success to you. You can do it. Every little step is a step towards success.

PARALEGAL

What is A Paralegal?

According to the American Bar Association (ABA)," a legal assistant or paralegal is a person, qualified by education and training or work experience who is employed or retained by a lawyer, law office, corporation, government agency or other entity and who performs specifically delegated substantive legal work for which a lawyer is responsible (1)." According to the Bureau of Labor Statistics, (BLS), paralegals, which are also called legal assistants, are carrying out more of the functions of a lawyer, but the ultimate responsibility is the lawyer's. Paralegals are not allowed to assume the responsibilities of a lawyer, such as set legal fees, present cases in court, or give legal advice (12). Some of the responsibilities of a paralegal may be to type contracts for the attorney to review, interview and screen potential clients, interview and screen witnesses, research laws and statutes, write briefs, organize evidence, file motions, etc. Depending on the area and the size of the firm will determine a paralegal's responsibilities. For example, in a small firm the paralegal may be responsible for assisting the attorney completely even answering the phone. However, in a larger firm, the paralegal may have his or her own secretary and only perform a small portion of the paralegal function working with several paralegals. In a smaller firm, the paralegal may perform all of the functions of a paralegal.

Paralegals can work for the government, a law firm or a corporation. The majority of paralegals work for a law firm. However, paralegals that work for a corporation enjoy better salaries and more benefits.

Educational Background for Paralegals

There are several routes you can take in order to become a paralegal. There are many different schools that offer various diploma and degree programs in Paralegal. Some schools offer a Bachelor degree in paralegal. Some schools offer an associate's degree or diploma programs. In addition, some receive on-the-job training with a law firm. For the most part, a typical paralegal has a degree either in paralegal or a degree in another field with a diploma/certificate in paralegal. Depending on a company's requirements, for the most part they do require you to have a degree in some form or another.

All schools are not created equal. In the sense that governing agencies, such as the American Bar Association (ABA) and some paralegal organizations, approve programs and they receive the distinction of being approved by those organization. The more prominent distinction is the ABA. Most law firms, corporations, and government agencies, may require that you have graduated from a school that has certifying credentials from one or both of these organizations. The ABA publishes guidelines that schools must follow in order to receive an approval from their organization (1).

The National Federation of Paralegals Association, (NFPA), offers a credentialing examination, Paralegal Advanced Competency Exam (PACE) for experienced paralegals, and is in the process of developing a Paralegal CORE (Competent, Organized, Responsible, Ethical) Competency Examination for those who may not be qualified for the PACE Examination (22).

In addition to the NFPA, the National Association of Legal Assistants, (NALA), offers a credentialing examination, which is also voluntary. The credentialing examination covers communications, ethics, legal research, judgment and analytical ability, and substantive law. In addition, they offer advanced certification examinations in contract management/contract administration, discovery, social security disability, trial practice, alternative dispute resolution, trademarks, personal injury and some others. For the purpose of this book as a small claims paralegal, most of these areas wouldn't have any relevance to the work that you may do in small claims (21, 22).

Areas of Law

There are several areas of law that you can specialize in as a paralegal. For example, there is family law, corporate law, bankruptcy law, estate planning and probate, litigation, real estate law, and intellectual property. There are other areas that are available, such as entertainment and sports management law, which will not be covered in this book.

Family law deals with family issues. It covers laws that affect a marriage and children. Some of the sub-areas include, divorce, child custody, child support, etc. This is an area that deals with family courts and laws that govern the family courts.

Corporate laws deal with business. Some areas include business formation, such as sole proprietorships, partnerships and corporations. It also deals with the laws that affect contracts, such as business entities. The definition of each type of business entity was discussed in the general section of business start-up in the previous chapter.

Bankruptcy laws deals with laws that affect lenders and borrowers. The three most prominent type of chapters that fall under bankruptcy laws: Chapter 7, 11 and 13. Individuals or companies who choose to file for bankruptcy usually are in severe financial trouble and need a way to either restructure their credit accounts, dissolve their debts or restructure their payments. Chapter 7 allows for the complete dissolution of debts owed to creditors, while Chapters 11 and 13 allow the restructuring of payments. Most other debts can be discharged and there will be a bankruptcy marked on an individual or companies file for approximately 8 years.

Estate planning and probate is an area of the law that deals with personal property, wills, and the distribution of those properties in the event of a person's death. Mostly wealthy individuals or families have large properties and expensive items that they would like to leave to certain individuals or organizations in the event of their death. However, no one is too poor to have a will, so you will find many individuals who are concerned about who will raise their children to who will drive their car. Wills prevent the government or courts from making the decision of how assets will be distributed for an individual.

Litigation deals with trials in courts. Litigation can cover criminal and civil court cases where there is a defendant, a plaintiff, a prosecutor and a defense attorney. These courts usually decide in criminal cases if an individual or company is guilty or innocent and usually, depending on the type of crime, decide if the defendant will pay a fine and /or go to jail. In a civil case, it usually is a case to decide if there will be some monetary compensation for a wrong that has been committed against a plaintiff. Courts will decide if there was a wrong committed and how much that individual (plaintiff) should be compensated.

Real estate law deals with the legal matters that govern all transactions of a real estate. It covers legal contracts between a landlord and tenant, the sale and purchase of real estate, and all other aspects of real estate.

Intellectual property deals with matters of inventions, patents, and creative works. For example, an inventor could use an intellectual property attorney to patent an invention that he or she just created. Also writers, musicians and poets all create original works that they want acknowledgement through copyrights. The Library of Congress usually handles the cataloging of copyrights and patents, where they maintain a copy of any literary work or invention as a way to establish legal rights to that owner.

Completing My Paralegal Education

I was well aware of the difference between attending an ABA or paralegal organization approved school, and a standard school that is not ABA approved. However, the one thing that attracted me to the school that I attended was its curriculum. At the time that I took the course my student loans from college had gone into default and I had no idea at that time what I wanted to do. So along with some other courses, I took the paralegal course, because it offered coverage in various areas of the law and it was very inexpensive. I took the correspondence course where I received my diploma in Paralegal Studies. It took me about four months to complete the course, and I was able to write some impressive resumes that covered each individual area that I studied, which was real estate law, corporate law, estate planning and probate, family law, bankruptcy law, intellectual property, and corporate law. Although the coverage of the areas was very brief, it gave me enough information as a foundation to learn about these different areas.

The school where I graduated was not an ABA approved school or approved by a governing paralegal organization. Although this was the case, in all my pavement pounding and cyber pounding, I was able to secure a few interview opportunities with a local area real estate agency. One of the things you have to realize when you graduate from a school that is not ABA approved is that you are competing with individuals who have gone to these schools. Just because you didn't graduate from an ABA approved school doesn't mean that all is a waste. This is where innovation and being creative come into play, and you too can create an opportunity.

Creating Opportunities in Paralegal

You've been knocking on several doors with your resume and no one seems to be answering. Do you just give up? Do you keep pounding the pavement or the cyber highway? I can tell you that I was really about to give up. I had always wanted to go to school for paralegal, which was one of my many interests, but I never pursued it and traveled down other avenues. I was really at odds with whether I wanted to go to law school or becoming a paralegal.

You should get a good book on the paralegal profession. One book, "Paralegal Career Guide," gives you information on traditional paralegal careers, as well as some of the nontraditional careers. The edition that I researched does not show small claims paralegal as of that edition. You can be assured that even if there are any individuals in this career, that there is probably only a handful. You would have to check in your local telephone directory for any listings. (16).

Have you ever watched the court shows on TV, specifically Judge Judy, The People's Court, Judge Mathis, etc? At times, have you noticed that there were individuals who didn't have all the necessary documents to complete their cases, and sometimes either the individual had to have someone from the office fax the document or they had to come back at a later date?

As you may already know, small claims court doesn't require that an attorney to be present. This could be a gold mine for a paralegal who wants to work independently and assist those individuals who want to file small claims against an individual or business. Sometimes, people don't always understand the full process of the courts and they don't know what questions to ask or what is required of them. How about creating an opportunity that doesn't rob a lawyer of a client? Because lawyers are not required in small claims court, this creates an opportunity for paralegals, who may have had trouble finding opportunities in the legal world.

The one thing with this creative opportunity is that you should not confuse your role as a paralegal by trying to give legal advice as a lawyer. Your job as a small claims paralegal is to only evaluate the person's situation and have that individual gather the evidence necessary to prepare their case for presentation in small claims court.

In addition to not giving legal advice, I believe that it is important not to create a conflict of interest. It is easy to get caught up in trying to get every client and thinking "money" instead of "ethics." One thing that could be damaging to your reputation is that both sides find out. This is an opportunity for more than one small claims paralegal, and it would be in your best interest to refer an opposing client to another small claims paralegal. The NFPA is made up of paralegal organizations and individual paralegals, whose purpose is to make a global presence of the paralegal profession in the legal community. According to the National Federation of Paralegal Association, there is a Model Code of Ethics and Professional Responsibility and Guidelines of Enforcement, which sets the stage of conduct within the paralegal profession (22).

What is so Cool about This Opportunity?

This opportunity is so cool because a fresh opportunity is being created that is not oversaturated, and it's a unique opportunity for paralegals. A lawyer can tend to the big stuff, and you, as a small claims paralegal, can tend to the small stuff, like small claims.

There are plenty of people who have never stepped inside of a small claims court, let alone any court and this could be a gold mine for the paralegal that can start a business in assisting those individuals. Some people think they understand the court system, and may not be receptive to your idea. However, if you and at least one other paralegal can get the word out about your businesses and how the both of you can help, the word could spread quickly. More than one paralegal needs to be established. You will never want to create a conflict of interest where you are helping to prepare both sides of the same case.

How Could You Go About Starting This Opportunity?

The first thing you will need to do is to assess if there is a large need for this type of service in your area. Do you come from a large or small town? If you are from a small town, there is a strong chance that a small claims paralegal is not necessary, but you will have to investigate this for yourself.

You find out that yes, there are a lot of small claims being filed and now you want to find out if there is any competition. You may have individuals that do this type of work, but may not call themselves small claims paralegals. This person or company is a potential competitor, so it is best to gather as much information as possible about your competitors. The more people or companies that are involved in this type of opportunity the less likely you will find a customer base. But, this all depends on the quality of service they are receiving, so it would be in your best interests to gather as much information about your competitor as possible.

You decide that you want to cash in on this opportunity and you want to be the first if there are no other individuals involved in it. You could be the envy of your town if you are able to create an opportunity that allows you to be the first to be involved. But, you have to be careful, because if you are successful, you will have others coming to rain on your parade. But, how fascinating would it be to be the first and be able to advertise that you are a small claims paralegal. This helps you to distinguish why you may charge a little more than your competitor.

Starting your business, you will have to decide whether you are going to create a sole proprietorship, partnership or a corporation. Go to the section on business start-up, which will explain the difference between the three business entities. In addition to deciding on the type of business, you will have to decide on a name and have that filed with the county clerk's office. For example, where I am from, you have to look through this large book of registered business names and ensure that the name isn't already being used. Once you have established a name, you will pay a fee to have that unique name registered to you. Once that is done, you will have paperwork drawn up depending on what type of business you will be establishing.

Essential to the scheme of things are a marketing plan and a business plan. These two documents will be used to present to potential lenders and/or investors for start-up or business capital to operate your business.

You will need to hire a bookkeeper or an accountant or you can do the bookkeeping yourself. However, it is important to have a professional review of your books periodically in order to ensure that you have the most complete and accurate books maintained. This is important, because you want to be able to track your expenses and losses, which could help with restructuring or getting rid of parts of your business that are not lucrative. It would help to establish a separate bank account so that your personal expenses will be separate from your business expenses.

You can create advertisement, business cards, stationary, etc., and start advertising your business. If your budget allows you to, you can have these items professionally done to present the best for your business.

It would be a good idea to have an area to take care of your administrative tasks. You will have to decide on whether to rent an office space or work from home. If you decide to work from home and don't want or need potential clients visiting you at home, you can make your meetings a luncheon date, where you can treat. Otherwise, you will have clients coming to your home. Also, if you can afford to, it may be a good idea to rent a post office box, especially if you are working from home. You don't want some disgruntled client coming to your home. If you are able to establish an office somewhere in town, this would definitely be ideal. It doesn't always reduce the dangers that may be associated with disgruntled clients, but it would provide a professional atmosphere that your client can respect. There isn't anything wrong with having a home office. There are ways to getting around to meeting with your potential clients and maintaining a very safe environment for yourself and your family.

There are several ways that you can solicit business for your small claims paralegal business. You can post a flyer. You can hand out business cards to random people. Always, when giving out business cards, let them know that if they know of anyone, please pass along the card. You can even hand one individual two or more cards or flyers, so that they can pass it along to a friend.

Invest in a good paralegal book for your reference. Although it may not give you information about a small claims paralegal, it doesn't hurt to understand the field. Read as much as you can about paralegals in general, and then find out more about the small claims court system. You want to display the confidence that you have been doing this job forever and are very knowledgeable.

Learn the do's and don'ts of your profession, and don't be afraid to ask questions. Do as much research as possible, and definitely attend school to get at least a certificate.

There are national organizations, as well as, state organizations that govern the paralegal profession in every aspect. For one, there are ABA approved schools, which allow you to sit for the Certified Paralegal or Certified Legal Assistant Examination. This two-day examination allows you to receive a certification of distinction. Also there is the National Association of Legal Assistants (NALA) and National Federation of Paralegal Association (NFPA). In addition, you should check with your state to see if there are any additional organizations available. If you have attended a school that is ABA approved or have a degree in Paralegal Studies, it may be to your benefit to become a member of these organizations.

Adding credentials of Certified Paralegal or Certified Legal Assistant, can add extra clout when introducing yourself to potential clients. Receiving this distinction at this time is not mandatory, and is voluntary. You will have to use your discretion when deciding whether to pursue this distinction or not.

Another great idea is to start a small claims paralegal organization. This is an excellent way to network with other small claims paralegals and get the information out there that this is another opportunity that is available to individuals who may be interested in working independently as a paralegal.

FITNESS

What is Fitness?

According to the Bureau of Labor Statistics, fitness trainers and aerobics instructors instruct and/or coach groups or individuals in exercise activities. People use varying levels of fitness to achieve different goals. For example, there is a person that may use fitness to lose weight, gain weight, body build, or maintain weight.

There are several types of activities that can be used to improve and maintain your fitness level. There are cardiovascular exercises that get the heart rate pumping. There is aerobics, running, jogging, jumping rope, etc. Also, there is anaerobic exercise, where weight lifting and nautilus equipment performs this type of exercise.

Educational Background

There are different educational degrees available for an individual who wants to enter the fitness field. You can earn a certificate/diploma or degree up to a PhD in this field. One can become a certified personal fitness trainer, where you are certified to help others become physically fit. You will be assisting them in reaching their physical fitness goals. For the most part, you are not required to have a degree to perform this job. Certifications do give you credentials which help you to stand out from the rest.

Areas of Fitness

There are three main areas of fitness are aerobic, anaerobic, and calisthenics.

1. According to the book, Fitness and Health, aerobic fitness is "synonymous with endurance or stamina. It describes part inherited and part trained, to preserve or persist in prolonged endeavors." It can also be defined as the maximal capacity to take in, transport, and use oxygen, which is best measured in a laboratory test called the maximal oxygen intake (or VO2 max) test (26).
2. Anaerobic on the other hand is the absence of oxygen; non-oxidative metabolism (26)
3. According to the website, About.com, calisthenics "refers to exercise that are done in a rhythmic, systematic way using the body weight for resistance. Typical calisthenic exercises include pushups, jumping jacks, squats and crunches and focus on building strength, endurance and flexibility (30)."

Completing My Fitness Education

Several years ago, I completed a certificate program in Certified Personal Fitness Trainer and Nutrition Specialist. It was more of an accident than anything else. At the same school where I was inquiring about correspondence courses, I was looking into the paralegal and the event/wedding planning courses. They had sent me the literature for the Certified Personal Fitness Trainer and Nutrition Specialist course. Because it was affordable and I have always liked working out, having a membership to a gym at one point, I decided, why not? It was an interesting course and I learned a lot about fitness.

I have struggled most of my adult life wanting to lose weight. I'm not morbidly obese, but I could stand to lose a few pounds. I'm one of those people who enjoys being physically fit. I like to jog, do aerobics, nautilus, and sports activities. Nutrition is one of my biggest weaknesses, because I don't always eat all of the right foods. Overall, I can say that the course was a great investment. I use to eat a lot of high cholesterol fast foods, but hopefully I will evolve into eating more well-balanced meals. Sometimes, I make efforts to eat better, but right now I have to focus on other things and the good fitness habits will follow. If you are someone who is very fitness-oriented, this could be a great opportunity for you.

Creating Opportunities in Fitness

I was able to come up with a unique opportunity which combines all of the things I love. If you are someone who likes to travel or wish you could, you could use fitness as a way of doing it.

When I was younger, I use to dream about traveling all around the world. This longing to travel different places and take pictures is what led me to wanting to plan fitness retreats. There are so many fascinating places that I would love to go to in the United States. Also, you could consider some great places such as Canada, Mexico, Turks and Caicos, The Bahamas, Barbados and Europe. The list is endless to the number of retreats you can plan.

You can plan on having retreats in a variety of themes. For example, to keep the playing field neutral, you can have a seniors' retreat, a married couple's retreat, or a single's retreat. By classifying these retreats, you have common people around the same age group and possibly the same fitness level doing the same activities, so that everyone feels a part of the program. The senior's retreat would allow people in the same age group and typical fitness level to exercise together.

Initially, you will not need a lot of equipment. But, if you can afford to purchase all the equipment for your customers, this would be ideal. However, if the group is renting bikes for a bicycle tour in a foreign country, you can allow each participant to rent their own bike. Some of the cheaper retreats to start off with are nature walks. As your business grows, then you can get into more expensive retreats. But the reality is that each individual customer would be responsible for paying their own expenses, but starting out with cheaper retreats can be an attention grabber and no one is investing money in something and not really knowing what to expect.

You can do many tours in the United States. Wouldn't it be exciting to take a hiking trip to the Rocky Mountains or go skiing in Colorado? The list is endless. The great thing about a fitness retreat is that it is not about exercising all day, every day. It is about taking an hour and making exercise fun. You can set up a typical day, where you can hold some classes in various exercise techniques, do some stretches then have an early morning workout, and then everyone can come back for breakfast or lunch. The rest of the day can be a day for the group to sight see or just go back to their room and relax. Doesn't this make exercise sound so much fun? No one has an obligation to exercise all day. They are allowed to take in the sites and take pictures and do whatever they like in exchange for an hour or two a day of exercise.

What is so Cool About This Opportunity?

One of the things that I have seen in others is that they don't like to exercise because they think of it as a chore. Me, I honestly love working out. I have purchased different exercise equipment throughout the years and have had gym memberships. I think it is fun doing things that really help your body to function better. I really hope that I get to the point where I really take the time to take good care of my body. For my age, I'm in okay shape, but I could be in better shape.

The purpose of these fitness retreats is to ease individuals into fitness. They will have fun doing it, and hopefully, they will continue to take the things that they learn and apply it in their everyday life.

I had taken a course in cosmetology and esthetics, in addition to the certified personal fitness training course. In addition, I had taken courses in fashion merchandising and design, and dressmaking and design. A typical day would have been on a weeklong retreat in the Bahamas. For example, everyone would wake up and we would have a morning class on exercise technique, have a morning stretch then we would do an exercise, whether it is a walk or a bike trail. Sometimes a bike trail or hiking trail might be done later in the day so that the group can catch the sites. They could take pictures. The whole idea makes everything sound more fun. We would come back and the group could go and do whatever they felt like, whether it is relax, site see, or go to the club.

The next day, they may have a class on skin care, hair care or nail care. These classes would be over a period of three days, skin care on one day, hair care the next day, and then nail care on another day. You could have the class during breakfast or maybe after exercising or before exercising. It really depends on time constraints and whatever seems to fit. Again, the rest of the day would be the group's time, and they are not obligated to do any exercise after that time or attend classes.

The retreat can be as fun as you want to make it. As I mentioned, I took some fashion and sewing courses which I had planned to sew different exercise gear that would be displayed and sold at the retreat.

I wanted to be a fashion designer when I was younger, and being able to combine all the things I love into one job is really exciting to me. Being able to teach people that exercise can be fun, and also show them how to take care of their skin, hair and nails; and show them also how to relax. This is one unique opportunity that just has so many great benefits.

The only places I have been outside of the United States have been Mexico and Canada. So the opportunity to travel with a group and do fun things together, yet not be bogged down with a strict schedule can really be a great vacation for those who need the relaxation.

There are so many great money making opportunities available with the retreat. A great way to take advantage of this opportunity is to obtain a certificate in travel and tourism. You can get a free trip out of this. If you can sew, you can sell people your exercise gear to start them out with fitness. Sometimes, what people may like, may not be available in the store. Wouldn't it be nice if you could create custom exercise wear that actually fits that individual? You can put together photo albums of the trip and sell them. Also with makeup and skin care products, if you sell for a particular brand, you can sell those items too. Or if there is a company that is willing to sponsor a portion of the trip in exchange for you to present their makeup or skin care products that is an idea too. This can be financially lucrative to you in many ways. It's nothing like being able to see the world and making money while you are doing it. If you have a background or love of photography, you could even take professional pictures on the retreat, and sell photo packets. You can really use your skills to your benefit to make this a fun and profitable vacation.

How Could You Go About Starting This Opportunity?

For an opportunity like this, I would say that depending on what you want to accomplish on the retreat, will determine what type of education you should obtain. For example, I wanted to teach basic exercise and nutrition, cosmetology and skin care, and relaxation. The certificates that I completed were certified personal fitness trainer and nutrition specialist, cosmetology and esthetics, and I would have completed a relaxation therapy course. This would qualify me to give talks in each area of interest. However, if you don't have a background in something that you want to cover you, could always hire someone that has that expertise.

My side gigs while on the retreat would have been photo albums, fitness wear and make-up, skin care and hair products. I would have compiled an album of the group engaged in different activities in addition to some of the sites where we visit. Of course, I would design a line of fitness fashion that I would have displayed during different meetings. They can place an order or I could sew a batch in the event that they wanted something during the time we were on the retreat. I would probably offer to sell some type of cosmetics (hair, skin and make-up). However, most people may use their own products, which they wouldn't be under obligation to purchase anything.

It really doesn't take much to start up this type of business. You would have to decide whether you want to make it a sole proprietorship, a partnership or a corporation. You would really have to assess the benefits and the disadvantages of each type of business and decide which one is more beneficial to you.

You really don't need an office per se, but it would be beneficial to have a computer. If you are going to design the flyers that advertise this opportunity, you will need a computer and a good quality printer. The most advertising that you would need to do is advertising your trip. If you plan the trip far enough in advance, you will be able to allow people to arrange a payment plan. This would be very beneficial in order to allow them to afford to go on the trip if they can't come up with the money in advance. Establish a cancellation window, because things do come up and people aren't able to go. If you have a window, they will know when they need to cancel. You should be gracious. Times are hard and everyone may get excited about the trip, and then realize they can't afford it. It will happen. Have an easy cancellation policy. If they don't make it this trip, then everyone can come back and tell them what a wonderful time they had, and they will wish they had gone. They can always make your next trip.

You should gather as many travel brochures to different places. The overseas trips can be a week in length, and the United States trips can be weekend retreats. Trips that are within the United States, you can make the group responsible for getting to the location, but make the hotel arrangements and the activity arrangements. Trips that are overseas I would collect the money for tickets and allow that to be your company's responsibility. The reason why you could make the

United States trips the responsibility of the group is that they can travel different modes of transportation. If they want to save money, they could travel by train, plane, bus, or use their own personal vehicle. However, if you want to charter a bus, that could be done with close destinations. You have to remember that it is a weekend retreat, so someone that lives far away from the destination would have to travel to your location in order to catch the bus.

With foreign travel, you could make the arrangements by making a group purchase. This may help reduce the rates. However, if this is something that you are starting, and you want to have people who come from different areas of the country, it may be more feasible to have them make their own arrangements. They would be more familiar with the airport that they are traveling from. However, I would put a clause in that makes them aware that they are responsible for making their own flight arrangements, and if they don't make it, but have paid on the trip, the fee or a portion of the fee is non-refundable. You don't want people using the excuse that they can't make it because they didn't make their flight arrangements. If at all possible, it might be more beneficial even if the individual lives outside of your area, to make all travel arrangements. This ensures that every person's travel arrangements have been made.

Have generic legal documents drawn up that specify the guidelines of the trip. If you have a legal document that tells an individual about the contract that they are entering and specifies the terms of cancellation, this would be legally binding in court in the event the individual tries to back out at the last minute or when it is too late.

You should be responsible for the exercise equipment. Some of the things you can start out with that are cheap are jump ropes; heart rate monitors, rubber bands, and mats if possible. These are things that you don't have to have right when you start out. But when you make your schedule of events, it would be helpful to get them just before the trip. You can have each individual carry their own jump rope and have them sign for the equipment and return it after you get back from the trip. You can type up legal documents that reflect that the equipment is in their possession and hold them legally responsible for damages or lost equipment.

I would consider that each person have some type of insurance in the event that they get sick. This makes the trip more secure in that you ensure that each individual is covered if they get sick in a foreign country. Some temporary coverage would be ideal for a situation like this.

To sum up everything, it is really a matter of just scheduling a trip as far as in advance as possible. You can create flyers and distribute them. You can also create a website advertising the trip. Have legal guidelines for cancellation that each individual will sign. You could type up legal documents and have them sign for the equipment and sign that they were returned. Your biggest responsibility will be just arranging the hotel and flight arrangements and the rent of a facility. You will gather your cosmetics, hair care products and the clothing line. This could be a really fun and rewarding opportunity.

Times when you are not traveling, you can do personal fitness training on your off hours. For example, I was going to schedule 12 trips a year, 6 week long trips, and 6 weekend retreats. My down time, I could be a fitness trainer. Also, if you have a group that wants to plan a retreat for them exclusively, you can do that also and charge them a special group rate. As requests for trips become more prevalent, you can schedule more trips, maybe 12 week long trips overseas, and 12 weekend long retreats. Depending on how many requests you get for group trips, you could leave time open for special events like this.

AUTOMOTIVE-MOTORCYCLE REPAIR

What is Automotive-Motorcycle Repair?

Automotive and motorcycle repair is usually done by a highly trained technician, who is able to fix various things on your automotive or motorcycle to keep it running smoothly. According to the Bureau of Labor Statistics, an automotive service technician inspects, maintains, and repair automobiles and light trucks that run on gasoline, electricity, or alternative fuels, such as ethanol. Motorcycle technicians repair and service motorcycles, scooters, mopeds, and small all-terrain vehicles.

Education Background

Although most community colleges offer an associate degree program in automotive repair, you can also complete a vocational school diploma course, and there are correspondence courses in these fields, which can provide either an associate of science degree or a diploma. (4). Training can take from 6 months to a year. Vocational schools usually provide intensive career preparation with in-class instruction and hands-on practice.

If you are someone who doesn't have the money or time to go to school for automotive or motorcycle repair, although it is not highly recommended, there are books that you can obtain that will give you valuable resources on how to repair a motorcycle or an automobile. For example, "Motorcycle Maintenance Techbook" by Keith Weighill gives you a breakdown of the servicing and repairs for scooters and motorcycles. In the book, it covers the tools needed, how to keep service schedule and records, engines, chassis, electrics, modifications and accessories. If you do decide to get a book, the library is a very inexpensive alternative, but it is better to purchase a book so that you can reference that book as long as you like (31).

As with automotive repair, if you are a do-it-yourself repairman, who can't afford to go to school, there are options where you can obtain books. "How to Repair Your Car", by Paul Brand is a layman's book, which describes step-by-step how to do basic repairs. One reason why basic repairs are good, because if you are seeking an opportunity in being a mobile repairman, without the equipment that a standard repair shop would have, you will only be able to do the basics. Major work requiring machinery, or special equipment would have to be taken to a repair shop where they will have to run diagnostics to find out what is the problem. The book teaches you basic troubleshooting, fuel systems, engine, electrical systems, cooling systems, drive train, suspension and steering, tires and wheels, brakes, and exhaust. Although this book covers a lot about automotive repair, it is highly advised that you take a course where you can be taught. Having an instructor to communicate whether via correspondence or in-classroom will help you to understand the field (2).

Those who train in this field can receive certification from the National Institute for Automotive Service Excellence (ASE), which is important for those seeking work in large, urban areas (4).

Currently there isn't an organization that covers motorcycle repair, but there is a host of organizations that are dedicated to riders of motorcycles.

ASE is a non-profit organization that works to improve the quality of vehicle repair and service by testing and certifying automobile professionals. For this test, they require that you have two years of hands on work experience. One year may be substituted if you have high school training, post-high school training or taken a short course in which you substitute two months of training for one month work experience. You may receive full credit for the two years if you completed a three to four year bona fide apprenticeship training program or completion of an OEM (Original Equipment Manufacturer) Co-op Program (23).

The general ASE Certification Tests offers more than 40 tests, which covers, cars and light trucks, collision repair, medium-heavy truck, truck equipment, school and transit buses, auto and truck parts. For maintenance and inspection program, the test covers Basic Automotive Maintenance. Refrigerant Recovery Program is for car and truck refrigerant handling procedures. These two areas are generally entry level certifications, which are also appropriate for students (23).

Areas of Automotive-Motorcycle Repair.

There are several areas in automotive-motorcycle repair, such as detailing, which you can provide painting and other designs to improve or enhance the looks of a vehicle. Also, there is engine maintenance and repair, and fixing fender benders.

Completing My Automotive-Motorcycle Repair Courses

This is an area, where I haven't explored, so I am only providing you with general information as a point of interest, if you are someone that doesn't mind getting your hands dirty. I have wanted to learn how to repair automobiles for my own personal use because it would have saved me money if I knew how to fix my own automobile, or when I am talking to a technician, I would understand what he is talking about for the most part it would be for my own protection.

Creating Opportunities in Automotive-Motorcycle Repair

Although there are various road side service plans, there may be limits to the number of times it can access it. How about offering people a mobile automobile-motorcycle repair service, where you can come to that individual and do minor repairs that do not require any shop attention? Many times when people require repairs, they are not within the vicinity of a repair shop or their vehicle/motorcycle is not operable. To be able to assist them, especially if they don't have roadside service, would allow them to get to the service station to take care of the larger repairs that you may not cover. You could also provide a service where you charge a monthly fee and provide unlimited service to an individual. You can also provide flexibility and provide a service on an as needed basis. It is really up to you and your availability. Always deliver what you advertise. If you want to provide a 24 hour service, but you know that you won't be able to provide a service during hours where you have other obligations, such as a full-time job, then you shouldn't advertise for that unless you have others who could service someone during these hours.

What is so Cool About This Opportunity?

If you are someone who is mechanically inclined and good with your hands, this opportunity will allow you to make an extra income, and provide a valuable and unique service to people in your community. Everyone can't afford some of the services that are provided by other plans that will service their vehicle. If you are fast efficient, and effective, you could build a great client list by word of mouth. It is very important in situations like this that you are fast and efficient. Once you have made enough money and have established yourself, it would be a good idea to hire others. You can't be in two places at the same time, so being able to get to people fast and efficiently is important in building a clientele.

How Could You Go About Starting This Opportunity?

If you haven't completed an auto mechanic or motorcycle mechanic course, you should first work on learning how to fix cars and motorcycles. Decide if you have the time to go back to a community college or technical school, or if completing a correspondence course is the ideal route to travel in order to gain knowledge in this field. The great things about community colleges are that it gives you well rounded knowledge in other areas that might be helpful in your career, such as communication and writing courses. Technical schools will focus more on the automotive courses, and less on liberal arts courses. However, with technical schools and sometimes the community colleges, you can be provided with valuable hands on training and internships, which allow you to work in that field. The advantages of a correspondence course are that you can finish at your own pace. I have taken correspondence courses, where I was able to complete the course in as little as four months. If you are looking to go into the career fast, correspondence courses allow you to go at your own pace. With a technical school it is more hands on and you will probably graduate with the tools needed to start working immediately. Outline the price for each service and the price for your various plans that you may implement in your business.

At this time, you can start handing out your business cards, flyers and brochures. However, your business is limited to your area. You will have to define the service area that you are willing to cover. Be mindful of the time it will take to get to that location and if it is worth servicing that area from your main location. Is it really worth traveling an hour to get to someone? Only if that person lives or work in your service area and has traveled outside of your area that you will still want to service that person. One complication is that a person who has traveled to another county or state. If you want, you can provide some type of service, where they pay you so much money per month so if their car stalls out of state, you can have some type of agreement with a service station in that area, and you may pay for it. Money that you receive for this type of service could be placed in an interest bearing account, and you would have to keep track of all payments to make sure that the customer is current. This pool of money can be used to pay for service fees. To cut down on costs, if this is not lucrative for you, you can put a cap on how much you will pay or reimburse for certain expenses. As you can see, it will be very important to decide what expenses you will cover and how much it should cost for each expense.

ARTS AND CRAFTS

What are Arts and Crafts?

The Bureau of Labor Statistics defines craft artists as individuals that make a wide variety of objects, mostly by hand, that are sold in their own studios, retail outlets, or arts and crafts shows. They work with a variety of materials, including ceramics, glass, textiles, wood, metal, and paper to create unique pieces of art such as pottery, stained glass, quilts, tapestry, lace, candles and clothing. Many craft artists also use fine-arts techniques, such as painting, sketching and printing-to add finishing touches to their art. According to the Merriam Webster dictionary, arts and crafts was a movement in European and American design during the late 19th and early 20th centuries promoting hand craftsmanship over industrial mass production. Arts and crafts can be a very relaxing hobby, and can also be lucrative. You will see many people sell their crafts online, at flea markets or on consignment at a store. There are so many opportunities in making money with crafts. It may not make you rich but the additional income can be useful. With some crafts, you have to have patience because not all crafts are quick and easy. Some crafts can take as long as a month to make, depending on how much time you spend on making it (3).

Educational Background

According to the BLS, there are programs in fine arts with a concentration in crafts arts. These programs provide an associate's, bachelor's or master's degrees in fine arts. In addition, local schools may offer various courses such as, pottery, knitting, crocheting, needlepoint, cross-stitch, scrap booking, knitting looms, drawing, painting and sewing. Some courses are a day long, while others may take as long as a month or more. This is one of the easiest ways to have fun, while you are making money (3).

There are several methods of learning arts and crafts. Some companies publish books that teach you certain crafts. For example, with knitting and crocheting, you can purchase a kit that starts you out with the supplies you need to complete the training projects that are presented in the book. There are some video instructions and other books that you can seek out that will train you in various crafts. Some arts and crafts stores provide workshops that will train you in knitting, crocheting, jewelry making, pottery, scrap booking and other arts and crafts.

Areas of Arts and Crafts

Pottery is the use of clay materials to create various objects, such as vases, bowls, etc., which can be painted. Pottery can be very messy having to use your hands to shape the clay, while it is spinning on the pottery wheel, but it can turn out some wonderful and exciting objects.

Knitting and crocheting are two crafts that require the use of yarn and needles to create various clothing items, household items, blankets, etc. With crocheting, you are using a needle of various sizes with a hook at the end to crochet items with various stitches. Knitting is the use of two needles with yarn. You will transfer stitches back and forth from one needle to the next until you create your desired item. In addition to using knitting needles, there are also knitting machines and looms. I believe knitting needles does give you better creative control, but knitting machines and loons are much faster in turning out your product.

Needlepoint and cross stitch are two arts and crafts that require the use of a cloth or board, and thread or yarn, which you use to form various patterns and pictures with the needle and thread or yarn. You can create wall hangings, bags, pillows, etc.

Scrap booking is arts and crafts that allow you to create memorable books of various activities and events. You can create birthday, children's sporting event or holiday scrapbooks, which can include pictures and decorations.

Drawing and painting is an arts and crafts form that requires the use of various mediums, such as ink, pencil, paints, and pastels, etc. Pencil and watercolor are usually done on paper, while oil and acrylics are usually done on canvas. You can create colorful art of various scenes. Most of my artwork that I have done is from various pictures that I found in magazines, books and on the Internet. To date, I have created over 200 pieces of artwork in various mediums. The unfortunate thing is that most of them have been lost.

Sewing is one of my favorite arts and crafts hobbies. I have always loved clothing and I like being creative. I have done most of my sewing with commercial patterns. Recently, I have sewn some skirts, dresses, vests, a jacket and a poncho by hand. My poncho has a matching hat and gloves. Because I don't usually fit the average clothing length, it is more convenient for me to make my clothing and make it to fit me specifically. I also have a lot of problems with the sleeves on coats, blouses, etc. Learning how to sew has been the most rewarding skill that I have ever learned.

Completing My Arts and Crafts Courses

There are some schools that offer a degree program in arts and crafts. I have been able to take individual courses in various areas, such as art, dressmaking and design, and photography. I completed my dressmaking and design course, but will eventually complete my art and photography courses.

Creating Opportunities in Arts and Crafts

If you do a search on arts and crafts organizations, you will find many different organizations. Some organizations are catered to different areas, cultures, etc. For example, there is an Indian Arts and Crafts Association, whose primary purpose is to support the ethical promotion and protection of authentic Native American art and culture. Another organization is the Arts & Crafts Movement Organizations and Societies, which gives a list of organizations and societies that are exclusive to various organizations devoted to arts and crafts. If you are someone who wants to have fun making money, while having a healthy and therapeutic job, then arts and crafts is a good opportunity for you. You can make such items as personalized pillows, blankets, paintings, greeting cards and posters.

During graduation, high school or college, a wonderful gift idea is a picture of an individual in their cap and gown, either in painting or pencil drawing. I actually did a 19" x 24" pencil drawing of me in my high school cap and gown, and two of me in my college cap and gown. You can also do paintings or a pencil drawing of weddings or birthdays. Also, I did a picture of me in my military uniform.

A greeting card idea is to personalize the card with drawings or paintings of the person that is being given the card. If you also have a knack for words you can include catchy greetings that really express your feelings.

What is so Cool about This Opportunity?

This is a cool opportunity because it is very therapeutic. You are able to combine your talent and create pieces of art that people will enjoy year after year. My favorites are the graduation and wedding paintings, and the greeting cards. With the right promotion and venue, you can turn this into a lucrative small business.

Being able to make knitwear and clothing is also very interesting. With a knitting loom, I have been able to create beautiful outfits, handbags, stuffed animals pillows, belts, etc. You can either focus on one kind of arts and crafts or expand your creativity among several arts and crafts. If you are unable to get to a local arts and crafts store, you can check online if you have Internet access. Craft supplies can be really inexpensive, yet create high quality items, which you can sell for a good profit.

How Could You Go About Starting This Opportunity?

If you don't have the skills to enter into this opportunity immediately, you will have to decide what interests you and how you would go about getting the training for the skills. Many crafts are very simple to learn and don't require for you to be in a class for a year or even a semester. Most classes are taught over several days, which is the nice part about learning a craft.

Next you want to decide on what materials you will need to start your craft business. Some crafts can be expensive but most are relatively cheap. If you have the time you can get ideas about various crafts just by looking at the supplies that are available in an arts and crafts store. You may want to develop an idea based on certain materials, and focus on that, or if you are someone like me that enjoys all arts and crafts, you may create projects and offer them for sale without having a general focus, such as creating handbags only.

Once you have your venue that you will use, you can start to advertise about your craft sales. I would get a camera to take pictures of each craft for advertising. If you can put together a catalog, you can offer it at the flea market or via mail and online to customers.

It's not likely that having an arts and crafts business will make you a millionaire. A smart way to sell them is to use more than one venue to sell them. In addition to renting a booth at a flea market or selling them online, you can sell them on consignment. I don't' think it is wise to just focus on one venue, if you want to make a lucrative income selling them.

COMPUTER FIELD

What is The Computer Field?

According to the Merriam-Webster dictionary, a computer is one that computes. In addition it states that a computer is an electronic device that can store, retrieve, and process data. The computer field is so vast, that it would take a book within itself to describe every aspect of it. For the purpose of this book, I will only tell you about the computer field that is in relation to my own idea. As you may have read, there are many people that are starting small businesses for various reasons. Some people want to experience their piece of the American dream. Other people want to work for themselves, due to layoffs, or lack of job opportunity. In relationship to this section, computer help desk can be an individual or a department that is devoted to assisting individuals or a group within a company with all of their computer problems, upgrades, networking, etc. For example in many large companies, they will house an IT department that will handle all the computer problems within that company. Some issues that may arise is to issue passwords to individuals, give permissions, update or implement new software, teach individuals how to use the software, solve any problems that an individual may have with operating the computer or using the software. According to the Bureau of Labor Statistics, which classifies help desk technicians as computer support specialist, defines them as "individuals that provide technical assistance, support and advice to individuals and organizations that depend on information technology (7)."

Educational Background

Working as a help desk personnel, you can go to either a technical school or a community college. For more advanced responsibilities, you would probably need at minimum a bachelor's degree. There are master's and PhD programs in computers. There are different areas, such as computer science and computer information systems. A help desk technician that works for a company usually receives on the job training, which can last a year or more. (7). There are opportunities to advance in this field to occupations such as computer programmers or software engineers (7).

Areas of Computers

As stated, there are so many areas of computer. Some people deal with hardware or software. Some people are network engineers or software engineers. Also, there is artificial intelligence, database management, and Internet.

Networks are a system of computers, peripherals, terminals, and databases connected by communication lines. Network engineers are individuals who keep the network connections maintained and compromised free. As data travels over a network, it can be accessed by outside sources. A network engineer's responsibility will be to make sure that these networks are secure.

Software is something used or associated with and usually contrasted with hardware. It can also be defined as the entire set of programs, procedures, and related documentation associated with a system and especially a computer system. A software engineer would be involved with developing and implementing computer software onto a system.

Artificial intelligence is the branch of computer science dealing with the simulation of intelligent behavior in computers. It is also the capability of a machine to imitate intelligent human behavior.

A database is a large collection of data organized especially for rapid search and retrieval as by a computer. A database manager would be in charge of maintaining this database.

The internet is an electronic communications network that connects computer networks and organizational computer facilities around the world.

Completing My Computer Education

I have worked in the computer field as a computer operator and did some database administration. I achieved a degree in computer information systems, but unfortunately, I was working in another field and was unable to gain valuable experience in computers. Although I love computers from a user standpoint, I would have loved to have the opportunity to work in the field and put my knowledge gained to use.

One of the areas of interest for me while working on my M.S. degree was to get involved with computer security. I thought it was fascinating the whole idea of keeping networks and Internet safe from hackers, etc. I wanted to specialize in this area at the PhD level, but wound up not being able to enter into the PhD program. I haven't worked with computers since receiving my degree other than being an end user.

Creating Opportunities in Computer

One opportunity that stuck out for me was to create an IT department at home that would help individuals and small businesses with their computer needs. Many times, people have various problems with their software, whether it is using a program or technical hardware problems. If you are someone with a lot of knowledge about computers, you could make some money in this field. An idea along with this was to offer a monthly subscription package that could offer either unlimited services, or smaller packages which offers so many hours of service or an as needed service for individuals or small businesses that may not use their computer as often. One thing that can make this lucrative is if you make yourself available 24 hours a day, seven days a week. This really allows those late night owls to have immediate access to your service. According to an article in Computer World, being in an organization and working as an IT help desk doesn't have much room for growth opportunity. In particular, help desk technicians can work in an organization where the IT professionals are separated from each other and can go 10 or 15 years without being promoted (9).

What is so Cool About This Opportunity?

This is such a cool opportunity for people who enjoy working with computers and people. You have to have patience and sensitivity when dealing with customers. Having knowledge of computers, sometimes we forget that people may have questions about things that may seem really simple to us because we are more knowledgeable. Being able to assist customers with their computers can be rewarding for the right individual. Sometimes, you may have to travel to the individual's home. One of the nice things you could offer with this opportunity is to research, purchase and install software to meet their needs. Of course, they would be responsible for the purchase price for the software, but taking on the task of shopping for them as well as fixing their computer can be really lucrative for you.

How Could You Go About Starting This Opportunity?

If you haven't already, you should obtain some training in computers. It could be in networking or computer repair. Most community colleges offer this major, or you can take a correspondence course that offers both an associate degree and a diploma course. The more you know, the more marketable you will be. Taking the extra time to complete a degree program will give you more of a competitive edge, because education really validates your knowledge.

Obtaining certain certifications would definitely make you more marketable. Certifications are tests that test your knowledge in certain skills. For example, there is a certification in Microsoft, such as the CNE (Certified Network Engineer). Also there are certifications in help desk, MS Word, Excel, Access, etc.

If the course doesn't provide you with computer repair tools, you should invest in the required tools to fix an actual computer.

You can generate a set of business cards, flyers and brochures to advertise your business. Being able to explain your skills and the type of business is necessary to get people interested in seeking your assistance.

It may be a good idea to have a vehicle or even a van in the event there are some computers that may need tools that you can't carry with you. You may have to take the computer home to complete the job. Have plenty of protective covering so that you won't accidentally damage any equipment.

BUSINESS

What is Business?

According to the Bureau of Labor Statistics, administrative management and general management consulting services firms, offer advice on an organization's day-to-day operations, such as budgeting, asset management, strategic and financial planning, records management, and tax strategy. Business can be defined as commerce or a company. The focus of this book will be on small businesses that usually operate out of someone's home (11).

Educational Background

You will definitely have a variety of course programs to complete your training in business from a diploma course to a PhD in business. Many people that are in charge of some type of company or in positions that require business knowledge, usually obtains an MBA (Masters in Business Administration) which provides them with leadership skills to run a business or a department. There are concentrations within business, such as finance, accounting, marketing, taxation, real estate, etc. Business is a very vast area of study, and usually at the MBA or MS level it is more specialized in a concentration (11).

Areas of Business

There are various areas of business. Some of them were mentioned in the previous section, such as marketing, accounting, finance, taxation, real estate, etc. Marketing is the area of business that advertises, sells and distributes a business and its product. Marketing is important, because you can have a good idea, but if you don't have a way of letting people know that you have the business, product or service, your business will not do very well.

Accounting is the aspect of business that keeps track of expenditures and revenue. Maintaining good accounting records is essential because it lets you know how your company is doing financially. It helps you to pinpoint areas that are not doing well, which you can choose to find ways of improving it or getting rid of it. Keeping good records is also good for tax purposes. When you have a business, you have to keep track of every expense and report it to the IRS at the end of the year or your business cycle. If you owe money, you will have to pay taxes, or otherwise you may be entitled to a refund.

Finance is the system that includes the circulation of money, granting of credit, making of investments, and the provision of banking facilities. Finance is an important aspect of business in that it helps your business to grow profitably. If you are able to manage the funds of your company properly, you avoid the pitfalls of going bankrupt or going out of business. When running a business, it is a wise choice to always invest your profits back into the business, especially in the beginning until your business grows and you are able to sustain paying yourself.

Taxation is the area that deals strictly with taxes of a business. It can be defined as the action of taxing, the imposition of taxes, revenue obtained from taxes, and the amount assessed as a tax.

Completing My Business Education

I have always been someone that liked to dabble with business ideas. It seemed at the time the only way to experience wealth and the American dream. I use to send away for countless money making opportunities on my quest to be successful and wealthy. But, the one thing about my business quest was that it was a means to an end. I needed money to pay for fashion design school, because at the time they didn't offer financial aid for the school that I wanted to attend. Money always seemed to be an issue when you have the passion and desire to have things in life and you are not wealthy. I completed a business administration associate's degree which I transferred to a four year college to major in accounting. Although I was not successful in completing my accounting degree, I gained valuable knowledge about business. Based on the education that I received I have been able to generate 15 business ideas, most of which are included in this book. I believe these ideas will be very lucrative. I was able to generate business cards, stationary, such as brochures and flyers to advertise my businesses.

Creating Opportunities in Business

One of the opportunities I came up with is becoming a small business consultant. If you are someone that has a business background, you can create a rewarding opportunity as a small business consultant. With the economy being the way that it is now, wouldn't it be nice to teach people how to be their own boss? The more you know, the more you can charge. You can file the paperwork to allow them to establish their business and obtain their license. You can help with creating a business or marketing plan. One of the keys to getting financial backing for a business idea is to have a great business and marketing plan. You can also advise an individual on the type of software they will need. Being a part of the entire business process would be ideal, because the more involved you are with a client's business, you are able to charge fees for your services.

If you did a search on small business consulting, you will find a lot of companies out there that do small business consulting, but at a different level. Most of these consulting firms help you with your day to day operations. What makes this opportunity so unique is that it helps with the implementation of a business idea, and with the whole start-up process.

What is so Cool About This Opportunity?

With employment opportunities being so dry these days, imagine being the one that saved a family from near homelessness, or helping to place a meal on their table. Being able to consult individuals interested in working for themselves would be a great opportunity. Most people don't know the procedures for actually starting the business and the required registration, documentation and licensing. If the individual is working, it would be financially lucrative to be able to take care of the things that would require that individual to take a day off of work. Being able to take care of paperwork, and assist that individual in all their business and financial needs would free up more time for that individual to continue in his or her job responsibilities if he or she is employed, while pursuing their dream of owning their own business.

How Could You Go About Starting This Opportunity?

First you would need to establish a business name for yourself. You can refer to the first chapter in this book, which pretty much covers the details of starting a business. Once you have done the preliminaries on your business, you can advertise, and contact various people that would be interested in your opportunity. You should make sure you give them a business card and a brochure that explains your services.

Once you start to get clients, you should emphasize to each client that it doesn't matter whether they have an idea of what they want to do; all they need is a desire to make extra money. If you have a creative knack of matching opportunities with an individual, based on their skills and an assessment of their interests, you could help them to come up with an idea that meets their needs and interests. You should also advise each individual that if they are not employed, they should obtain a job at least part-time because with business, it is not a steady flow of income in the beginning. Sometimes it can take as much as three years to see a profit. So, if you are advising them of the situation, they will not have unrealistic expectations. It is very important to not make them think that they are going to a millionaire overnight. Being in business takes hard work and each individual has to work hard to make their business marketable. Being honest with them about business is very important. If they don't have unrealistic expectations, they will not have a reason to bad mouth you and give you a bad reputation to other clients or potential clients.

Offer to work with them during the year for a fee of course. You advising them along the way can give an added boost and help them to make their business grow. You can emphasize how important it is to have someone consulting them in order to give them good advice on how to run their business.

BROADCASTING

What is Broadcasting?

Broadcasting is the transmission of a program or some information by radio or television. If you ever dreamed about being in front of the camera and have good camera presence, you could possibly be the next big thing on television, radio, and now even the Internet. According to the Bureau of Labor Statistics, web site or Internet producers, which are a relatively new occupation in the broadcasting industry, plan and develop Internet sites that provide news updates, program schedules, and information about popular shows (9).

Educational Background

There are degree programs in journalism/broadcasting, film and video, but the areas that will be covered in this segment are more for the amateur videographer. It would be up to you to try to make high quality and professional looking videos if this is something that you plan on pursuing on a professional level. There are also diploma courses in broadcasting, but if you are good with a video camera, you could possibly learn on your own.

Areas of Broadcasting

There are many areas you can cover in broadcasting, such as news, TV, reality shows, talk shows, etc.

With news, you can sponsor an online web news show, that covers your area, or you can pull news off the Internet. TV and reality shows can be made in order to cover a topic of interest. For example, I have ideas for reality shows, such as "The Weight Loss Journal," "In Search of My Heritage," "The Style Show," and others, which I hope to, begin soon.

Completing My Broadcasting Education

I haven't completed any broadcasting courses. I have taken photography courses, which have covered some of the things that you would find in a video/broadcasting course. I plan to get my camera and go.

Creating Opportunities in Broadcasting

What if you could create a hit reality show that can be scheduled every week? Depending on the quality of the show, this could be your calling card that will get you in the door. You can do talk shows, information shows, or a reality show. Some of the ideas can begin with things that are going on in your life. I have come up with over 10 ideas for reality web shows that can be broadcasted on Internet websites. I was able to capture future events that I had planned, and capture issues that I want to address, to make many different shows. The key is to schedule the show at the same time every week. I have a website, where if an individual misses a show, they can come to the website and view the previous recording. I hope to be able to set up the previous recordings so people can see them over and over again if necessary. Some of my ideas have been related to planning my wedding, having a baby, breaking into the modeling world, climbing the corporate ladder, and searching for my birth father and his family. You can look into your own life and find various ideas that could be turned into a reality show or even a talk show. When you think of ideas, find something that has some longevity to it. For example, searching for my heritage or breaking into the modeling world takes a lot of work that can be documented over several shows. Climbing the corporate ladder is something that can take years if you are starting from the bottom. People like things that have a lot of suspense, especially when they are wondering what will happen next? If you are a creative person, you can come up with some great ideas just based on your life.

What is so Cool About This Opportunity?

This opportunity could make you famous. It can get you through the door and on TV. This can lead to an exciting career as an actress or actor. If your content is interesting, you could get a large following of people. With that in mind, you may be able to contact various companies, who may be interested in you advertising their products on your show. This could lead to extra cash in your pockets. This could also lead to your own show. If you can put your best foot forward, you can really make a small investment of time and effort to give the best quality picture possible into an opportunity that could make you some good money and a star.

How Could You Go About Starting This Opportunity?

According to the article, "How Can I Broadcast a Live Web Show," there are several easy-to-use solutions for broadcasting live video. For example, there are several websites, such as UStream.tv, Stickam.com and YouCams.com (27).

Ustream provides you with a video player than can be embedded right into your website or personal blog for live webcasting. Stickam. com allows you to create live web video shows right from your browser and have video chat sessions. YouCams.com allows you to do live shows for a select group of friends or colleagues.

First thing to do is to come up with an idea about a show that would have some longevity. For example, you want the show to run as long as possible with fresh ideas that could be aired over a long period of time. Some things you could stretch out a bit, but you have to keep in mind whether the idea is going to keep the viewer interested. I believe that my idea, searching for my heritage is interesting because it is so unique. My story has interesting content, because although I know my father and I know of his children, I never met his family. I never knew where he lived or much about his family life. In turn, I don't think his family knew about me either. So, the challenge will be is trying to locate him and/or his family members, and also discovering his heritage. So as you can see, that it's not a matter of me knowing his address and knocking on his door. I have some things that I have to do to locate him and his family, so this idea is something with longevity.

Once you have developed an idea, you want to get props to record and air your show. If you have someone who can operate a camera for you, then you can probably get a more professional quality camera, depending on your budget. For me, I will be the sole proprietor of my show, so I found a camera that allows you to self-record. The camera quality is adequate, but the important thing is that I am able to place the camera on a tripod, and start filming. I placed the camera on the highest quality picture, which takes up a lot of megabytes. The higher the quality of your picture, the less time you will have to actually run your show.

Other props that you will need are really in your presentation. You should invest in make-up, a hip wardrobe, manicure, pedicure, hair style, etc. Putting your best foot forward every time is very important in making a good impression. Looking impeccable and stylish will bring a good impression about your show. Try to test the camera to find your best side. For example, you want to be able to position yourself so that you always look good in the camera. If you have several sides that look attractive, for example your profile, you should film all of your good sides. You don't want to look monotonous in your video. But remember, to never film your bad side. If you have to keep doing your show over and over again, that would be ideal in order to get the best picture. I would recommend that before officially airing a show that you complete at least 10 segments, so this will give you time to record the next segment. In the event that you have to redo a show, you will have at least 10 weeks to record that particular show. Don't do a show a week, because if there are problems, you will have time to address them before the airing of the show. You don't want to advertise your show for a certain time, and because you don't like the way that the segment turned out, you wind up missing a week of the show. Be a person that delivers quality all the time and on time.

Make-up is essential for men and women. Make-up enhances your beauty, and camouflages any defects. If you don't know how to put on make-up, you can easily go to a make-up counter at a major department store, where they have people who can teach you how to apply make-up for free, and they can help you select the colors that are right for you. In addition, you could take a course or you can get a book on make-up applications and learn how to apply make-up for your particular facial structure. I personally completed a correspondence course in cosmetology and esthetics, where I learned how to apply make-up, hair styling and care, nail care, and skin care.

An appropriate wardrobe is essential in delivering the total package for your show. For example, I want to do a show that chronicles my weight loss, so it would be important for me to wear exercise clothes. I wouldn't wear a business suit, and I wouldn't wear a lot of make-up for an exercise show, whereas, my show that will deal with my climb up the corporate ladder or as an entrepreneur, I would wear more professional clothing. A sweat suit wouldn't be appropriate for this type of show. Always think clearly what will be appropriate for the show and stick with what is best for the show. You always want to deliver a well polished, appropriate and professional image in each situation.

Always be well groomed. You can get away with having well polished nails. They don't have to be extra long, just well maintained. Although your show may not deal with you showing your feet, having a total look of a good manicure and pedicure could really help you feel good psychologically. A segment, you may want to wear sandals, so it would be appropriate to have a good pedicure. If you don't have pretty feet, then this would be an area that you wouldn't want to include in your taping. Always tape your best features unless you are doing a show about feet.

Your hair should be appropriately styled for the show. If you are doing a business related segment, then you want a natural color for your hair, and an appropriate style for the segment. For something more casual, you could probably get away with being a little more eccentric, but make sure that it is appropriate for the show.

Find a nice quiet area where you will be able to talk into the camera without being interrupted. You really need to have a clean, neat space where you are able to film your show. If you have a spare room, that could be an ideal place. A cheap way to create your set is to get table cloths that can be used as a back wall. If you have a table to sit at and record your show, that would be ideal. This would be a great place to include any products that you are endorsing. Before trying to get any endorsements, you should wait and work hard to get a good following of the show. This is leverage to bargain for more money for the endorsement deal. If you are doing an area that involves an exercise segment, it will be important to have a large area where you can demonstrate different exercises. Most other segments you wouldn't need as much space. Having a small table and some props may be the only thing that you need.

After you have located the space that you will be using to record your show, you will need to focus on what kind of camera you will want to use. There are many cameras available on the market; you will have to do a little research into the best camera to meet your needs. Because I don't have anyone to actually operate the camera, I purchased a Vivitar 410, which has a swivel screen so that you can actually see yourself in the camera. This allows me to see what I am filming. The picture quality is adequate. I have my setting on the highest quality picture, which doesn't give me as much time to record as it would if I placed it on a lower setting, which is standard with all cameras. The camera is less than $50. You have to purchase a separate SD card, which I purchased an 8 GB SDHC card. Cards with more gigabytes are available up to 32 GB or more. Eventually, I will invest in a larger card. You should get what is in your budget.

You need to decide how long you want the show to run. I think that for a web show that 15 minutes or less is ideal. You can type up scripts and time yourself to see if you reach your goal time. It is important to not have a web show that is too long. There is so much to do on the Internet, that having a show too long may not captivate your audience for the entire show. Having interesting content may draw people to your show if it is long, but showing 15 minute segments will probably ensures that people will view your show from beginning to end. Again, you should definitely prepare at least 10 scripts of what you are going to say. You can time yourself reading the scripts, and after you have made adjustments to lengthen, shorten or modify your script, you can present a final script. Make sure your script is well polished. Speak slowly with a clear speaking voice so that what you are saying is understood by your audience. Also, you should speak loudly, so that your voice is being recorded clearly.

Once you have written at least 10 good segments, you are ready to tape your show. Sometimes the slightest imperfection can mean a lot, so you may have 99% of your segment with good content and one flaw. If it is really noticeable, I would re-record. However, there may be editing software that you could use that you could modify that particular portion. You would have to research what is out there and decide if this is possible. If the segment is important, you may be able to re-do that particular portion and just edit it into the rest of the segment, but it is extremely important that you make a good impression every time you air. Rushing to get something aired and not thinking about the quality of the segment can mean a failure in your show. Always strive to achieve above and beyond, even if it means to re-record your segments 100 times. You always want to present your best every time.

Now that you have recorded at least 10 shows, you have more time to work on future shows. Continuing with your segments, you will have more time to record future shows, but don't procrastinate. Now that you have 10 or more weeks of shows, you should work hard to be fast, effective and efficient. Try to record as many, high quality shows as possible. Being able to crunch out many quality shows, will give you more time to focus on other things, like possibly generating more ideas for other shows, contacting and working out agreements with different sponsors, gathering additional props, etc.

There are many ways to increase your shows viewing. For one, you can use social networking sites. It may be a good idea to keep a website where if people can't watch your show at a particular time, they can go to your website and view the show at their leisure. Also, they may want to re-review a show that you aired. This is all possible if you keep a history of the shows that you have recorded. You can also print flyers to advertise your show and post them or hand them out to people. If you don't mind your co-workers knowing what you are doing, you can even let them in on your show.

You have a large following of people, so now you are ready to contact sponsors to get them to advertise or sponsor your show. This is a good way to add an income. You will have to find companies that are appropriate for the shows that you are creating. For example, for an exercise show, you could possibly contact a sneaker company, or a company that makes exercise clothing. If you are following a particular diet, you could contact that company to see if they would sponsor your show. Certain diet foods, the list is long of sponsors who could help you out. For a business show, you could wear particular designer clothing, maybe a food company or a beverage company. This particular show would be limitless as far as whom you can contact.

You really need to think about the layout and setting of the show and how that company's product can be implemented into your show. It really needs to make sense, so that your audience is sold on your endorsement of that product.

If you are someone that started out on a budget, you may want to eventually upgrade. You could probably start out with a small investment, but eventually, you may want to upgrade your equipment to more high quality equipment. This could be a great way to be discovered, but be realistic about the chances of it making you a big star. You should have fun doing it. One of the things about being discovered is that there is a possibility that you will lose all creative control. Doing your own show, it allows you to use your ideas and your creativity. When someone else is running the show, your input may be nil to none, but you will probably receive a salary that is more than what you are making with your current self-broadcasting. I think the most important thing is to enjoy doing it and have fun with it, and if it happens, be prepared.

You're a hot star and everyone is recognizing you. Always maintain a professional and courteous image. Be ready for the paparazzi or adoring fans, you never know who is watching you. Don't let the stardom go to your head, give an autograph when requested. Watch your star shine.

COSMETOLOGY

What is Cosmetology?

Cosmetology is the study of the skin, nail and hair. It is the art of caring for these areas of the body. It is not as involved as dermatology which is the study of the skin and its functions. Cosmetology is more about adornment and pampering, having your nails or toenails manicured, cleansing and applying makeup on the skin and styling the hair. According to the Bureau of Labor Statistics, a barber and cosmetologists' focus on providing hair care services to enhance the appearance of customers (25).

Educational Background

Cosmetology is a diploma course that takes approximately nine months full-time to complete. Currently, there are no degree programs for cosmetology, which is not a requirement. In the cosmetology course you will learn certain portions of the parts of the skin, layers of the hair, and nails; however the primary structure of the course is to understand how to style hair, take care of the skin, and adorn the nails. If you are someone who enjoys working with people and pampering them, this could be a very lucrative field for you. Once you have completed the course, you will be required by your state to take a licensing exam for cosmetology. You are only eligible to take the exam if you have graduated from an accredited instructor-led school. You should check your state to ensure what the guidelines are prior to going to school. Some states require that you train so many hours before you can sit for the licensing exam. According to an article on About.com, an individual must attend a state-licensed barber or cosmetology school and be at least 16 years of age (25). Once an individual has completed training, they usually must take a state-administered licensing exam (25).

Areas of Cosmetology

As noted, there are several areas that one could specialize when becoming a cosmetologist. For example, there are some that exclusively style hair. They may perform such functions, as wash, set, permanents, chemical relaxer, coloring, body wave, or haircuts. There are some who may specialize in just coloring, which is considered one of the more difficult areas of styling hair. (20).

Some cosmetologist may specialize in nail care. The range is from a basic manicure to adding tips or some stylish nail art. This is a very creative field, because you can paint the nails with different designs and colors. Nail art can be as beautiful as a tattoo, and can be lucrative if you have the art skill to make creative designs. A nail technician course isn't as long as a cosmetology course in that it doesn't require as many hours as the cosmetology course. But, if you are interested in having a well rounded education, the cosmetology course does cover some aspects of the nails, but not as in depth as the nail technician course by itself (20).

The area of cosmetology that covers skin care is call esthetics. If you wanted to specialize in skin care only, the esthetician course is actually longer than the cosmetology course. Again, taking up cosmetology it will cover some aspect of skin care, but not as in depth as the esthetician course. In both courses you will learn about the different layers of the skin, different skin types and how to care for each type, make-up application, and how to evaluate a person's hair, skin and face shape to determine make-up application and color application (20).

Completing my Cosmetology and Esthetics Diploma

When I first came across a home-study course in cosmetology and esthetics, I was very curious about its quality and content. While in high school, I always did other people's hair and my own, and I don't think that there is anything that I hadn't quite sampled as far as relaxers, perms, and a few hair colors.

This had been the first time I saw a home-study course in cosmetology and esthetics. I knew that the course would not allow me to sit for the licensing examination, but the curiosity was overwhelming me.

This course was excellent in that it provided you with the textbooks that a typical cosmetology course would provide. But, because the course is not instructor led, you may not be eligible to sit for the licensing examination. The real fortunate thing about completing this course is that I went to the library and ran across a book that helps you prepare for the licensing examination; I was able to answer the majority of the questions. I was able to learn enough to be able take the examination. You would still be required to attend an accredited school, but you would be just that far ahead of the rest of the students. I really enjoyed the course and all that it taught me. Although we didn't quite make a career connection, for financial reasons, I decided that it would be lucrative in other ways. For example, in the chapter on fitness, I explained how I could use the knowledge that I gained from this course to offer a training class in hair, skin, and nail care, on a fitness retreat.

Creating Opportunities in Cosmetology

One of the unique opportunities for someone with a diploma in cosmetology and esthetics, but not a license would be to service the individuals who are homebound. For customers, who are not able to bet out of the house, but would like to keep their looks up, a cosmetologist, who has the knowledge, yet not the license could do basic hair care, nail care and skin care. For example, because you are working within someone's home, you will probably not be able, by law, to work with chemicals and dyes for the safety of both you and your customer. However, you may be able to wash, cut, and set someone's hair. You can also do mini facial and basic manicures. You would have to check with the state licensing boards to understand the full requirements that a cosmetologist should follow.

There are disadvantages to not working in a salon. For one, salons may be a more organized and neat and can be adjusted to your comfort. You can have some customers who are able to come to your home. However, the ones that are homebound would have to be serviced at home. You really have no control over that individual's environment. If you are a licensed cosmetologist, you may not make as much money as you would if you were working in a salon. It is more convenient to have a customer come to your home, instead of going to that individual's home. Your salon booth is geared to have everything organized in order to complete the job. However, you would have to check your local and state zoning laws about running a business from your home and working in someone else's home.

What is so Cool About This Opportunity?

What makes this opportunity so cool is the fact that you will be working alone. You can flex your hours and get up as late as you want. It is flexible enough that if you want to do other things, such as going shopping, doctor's appointments, etc., you can schedule your cosmetology appointments around your other appointments.

If you are someone that is truly into beauty, it is the opportunity to do what you love. You can go from a basic manicure to the fancier artwork. They now have available the nail art pens, which makes it easy to be artistic in doing someone's nails. If you are someone with artistic abilities, you could do very well being a nail technician. However, when it comes to making manicure and pedicure service available, nine times out of ten, a person that is invalid and shut in will be senior citizens, and they will probably just want a basic manicure. However, this is an idea that can generate a clientele. This can be your side gig.

As far as facials, everyone could use one every now and then. Facials may be a little difficult when dealing with people in their homes. They may have a small bathroom, although the kitchen may work. It is a lot different than working with the nail and hair, because the face needs to be submerged in water. You could in fact use a facial steamer to replace the need of washing the face in a sink.

How Could You Go About Starting This Opportunity?

If you haven't already taken a course in cosmetology, you can look into local schools. Most schools take about a year to complete full-time. Upon completion, you can take a test to be licensed as a cosmetologist. Depending on what you want to do, you could also complete a correspondence course in cosmetology. However, it may not lead into you becoming a licensed cosmetologist, and you would have to check with a school to see if they will accept the credits from the correspondence school. Some states may allow you to apprentice with a licensed cosmetologist.

Once you have completed your course of study, you can seek work experience in someone else's salon for a period of time. You may want to eventually become salon owner or you may want to get started in the unique opportunity presented in this book.

If you have all the tools you'll need, you can start in an opportunity to provide hair, nail and skin care to people who may be house bound and can't get out. I know you may be wondering why someone would want to care about looking good, when they are home bound. Sometimes looking good can be therapeutic, and although these people can't get out, they are sometimes at home and depressed. Being pampered can make that person feel better. Besides, they may have parties or guest over and want to look their best. So, believe it or not, this can be a lucrative market. You really don't have to limit your clientele to just people who can't get out. Sometimes, people just don't want to go out. Why not bring your service to them?

You can begin to get together business cards, flyers, and possibly brochures. You will have to find various venues to advertise your service. You will also have to map out your travel area. For example, are you willing to travel for hours to get to a client? When you think about the cost of gas, time, you will have to decide whether it is worth traveling for 2 hours to get to a client. The closer you concentrate your area to your main base, the shorter time you will spend traveling to those places, and the more clients you can see in one day. If you have a client that is two hours away, you will spend at least 6 hours with one client. You will spend 4 hours in travel and an hour or two servicing the client. This will take up valuable time that could be used servicing other clients.

Working exclusively with clients in their home is a great way to earn a good income. You can work from home, in that you maintain your supplies, books, and any administrative work, such as appointments, and supplies. It may be wise to have space so that you can get your supplies ready the night before, and keep an appointment book in order to keep your appointments and days organized.

For this type of job, it is more convenient to have a vehicle to carry supplies and to get to your appointments as quickly as possible. If you don't have a vehicle, you can possibly get away with having a smaller travel area. Some areas offer a type of car sharing service, or you can get a car rental or a cab. You will have to assess the financial benefits of having this type of car or utilizing a car rental or a cab. If you live in an apartment complex, you could possibly work within that apartment complex and the surrounding area. Check for laws pertaining to running your business from home.

Whether or not, you are able to establish this type of business opportunity, would be up to the states regulatory committee that oversees the licensing of cosmetologist in your state. Many salon owners are required to carry insurance that covers malpractice, premises liability, fire, burglary and theft, and business interruption. Because you will be working in either your home or someone else's home, you will need to know what services you will and can provide and if insurance is necessary (25).

COOKING

What is Cooking?

The Bureau of Labor Statistics classifies individuals, who are professionals in this industry as chefs, head cooks, and food preparation and serving supervisors that oversee the daily food service operation of a restaurant or other food service establishment. According to the dictionary, cooking can be defined as cuisine, cookery, baking, food preparation or food. To cook is to prepare, make, put together (10).

Educational Background

Although there are degree programs at a community college, you can also obtain a certificate from a formal chef school or through a correspondence course. Some people have old family recipes that are handed down from their parents, and are pretty much self-taught. A growing number of chefs participate in training programs sponsored by independent cooking schools, professional culinary institutes, 2 year or 4 year colleges with hospitality or culinary arts department or the armed forces (10).

Areas of Cooking

There are several areas of cooking to include the type of cuisine, such as American, Southern, Mexican, etc. There is also cooking deserts, wedding cakes, meals, etc. Depending on your desire, you can specialize in a type of desert, wedding cakes, or meals. There are many opportunities to make money in most of these areas. You can help with fundraising at a local church or school, planning meals, bake sales, or some other type of cooking venture.

Completing My Cooking Courses

I don't have any formal training in cooking. I have taken a cooking class in high school. My mom doesn't cook anymore, but she was a great cook and I remember these huge dinners she would prepare for the holidays. The apartment was filled with the scent of various foods. Holiday times around my mother's house meant good eating. When I lived in Kentucky, I prepared my own meal using some of my mother's recipes. I couldn't afford a big dinner, and unfortunately it was just me, so one Thanksgiving holiday, I purchased some Cornish hens, yams, sweet potato pies, collard greens, and macaroni and cheese. I actually love cooking, but it's much more fun when you are preparing meals for your family or guests.

I can prepare many different types of desserts and meals. I love baking cakes, brownies, cream pies, lemon meringue pies, banana pudding, cupcakes, cookies, and bread puddings. As far as meals, I can bake and fry chicken, hamburgers, steaks, various poultries, meats, vegetables, homemade macaroni and cheese, corn bread, as well as many other items. I haven't tackled seafood, which I truly love. I have never cooked fish or shrimp.

Creating Opportunities in Cooking

With this fast pace society, there are many people that don't have the time to prepare meals, whether it is dinner or a lunch. Traditionally, people that get involved with cooking usually cater for parties or gatherings. A unique opportunity would be for the busy parent who works and doesn't have time to prepare meals for her children. You can be one to prepare meals that can be placed in microwaveable bowls and prepare meals for a week for families. The male who never learned how to cook, you can prepare three meals a day to include a bag lunch that includes nutritious food. You can prepare meals to meet special needs, such as, diabetic meals, low sodium, low fat, vegetarian, or vegan; the list is endless. There are people out there who don't have the time to prepare meals for their families or themselves. You can be the one to cash in on this unique opportunity.

What is so Cool About This Opportunity?

Eating out two to three times a week can get very expensive. If you can find a happy medium between cooking meals for busy families and eating out, you can save this family a lot of money by preparing their meals and make money. For example, if there is a family of four where two children goes to school and both parents work, preparing 12 meals a day at a rate of of $3-$5 per meal, could calculate to approximately $36-$60 dollars a day or $252-$360 for a seven day week, or $180-$300 per week for a five day week. The one thing about these prices, you may want to take into consideration the cost of food. Maybe providing a shopping service will help to pick and prepare the foods. This seems like a lot, but if you are providing a family with healthy foods, and three good meals a day, it may be worth it to a busy family, who doesn't have the time to prepare meals or shop for food. Think of the fact that a family that doesn't prepare meals and eats out. For a family of four, the family may spend on average $100 a day or $700 a week. A breakdown of these figures is the family eats every meal out. On average, they may spend about $30 on breakfast. For lunch, they may give the kids $5 each ($10) and the adults would spend $10 each ($20), and for dinner, they may spend about $40 for the four. Adding this all up, a family would spend about $100 per day, or $700 per week for a seven-day week, and $500 a week for a five-day week. With your meal preparation service, they would be spending $36-$60 a day. You would be saving this family $40-$64 a day or $200-$448 per week at the most. According to the Bureau of Labor Statistics, approximately 8% in this field is self-employed.

How to Get Started in This Opportunity?

First you need to find out if there is a need for your services in your neighborhood. I think with any type of business, you will want to know that there is a definite demand. You can begin by talking to neighbors or even friends, and observe different trends. You can conduct a survey and mail them out to a neighborhood to ask potential customers if they have a need for this service.

If you can get additional training, this would be great. Having a well-rounded menu plan of various cuisines can broaden your market.

You can obtain training through correspondence courses if you don't have the time to go back to a traditional school.

Once you have talked to these individuals, the ones that say they would consider this type of service will serve as your initial mailing list. You should create a flyer and mail it to the customers who responded yes to your meal preparation service. Another place to hand out or even hang up flyers is at your local supermarkets. Imagine a customer seeing your flyer while they are shopping for groceries. The fact that you would provide this service would probably pique their interest.

How many clients can you handle would be your next determination. Remember you will have to determine how much cooking you want to prepare. Some people may want a 21-meal plan, 15-meal plan, or maybe a lunch or dinner plan. With this in consideration, you will really have to work hard to prepare these meals on time, so that they will have the meals for the week. If you could hire additional workers, that would be helpful.

If you don't want to do the meal plan preparation, you may want to consider pastries. You can make cookies, wedding cakes, and cakes for different occasions, pastries, and many different things. You can offer these items as part of an organization's fundraiser. There is so much you can do.

You can work from home. You should ensure that you have a very clean and safe environment. You should ensure that you keep your hands clean or work with disposable plastic gloves. It is really important that when you are working with food preparation, that you are not passing germs onto others. Keeping your area sanitary will ensure that your clients are given clean and well-prepared food that won't make them sick. Keeping a bottle of hand sanitizer and constantly washing your hands ensures that things are clean and safe.

One way to take on many clients is to prepare a menu of foods that you may be cooking for the week. You can provide each client with a menu and they can decide what meals they want. If you stick to a weekly meal plan that consist of what you are offering for the week, this will allow you to take on more clients, because it is easier to prepare in bulk the same type of food for several clients. You will have to use your discretion, based on your surveys to determine which plan is the best plan to meet the needs of your customers.

How Could You Go About Starting This Opportunity?

If you haven't already done so, think about getting training in cooking. Once you have completed your training, you will have to establish your business entity.

Think about the type of foods you would like to prepare, or a specialty that you would like to provide. For example, maybe you want to bake or do breakfast and lunch, cupcakes, desserts, etc. Once you have established your niche, you will want to get the word out that you are in business.

DESKTOP PUBLISHING

What is Desktop Publishing?

According to the Bureau of Labor Statistics, desktop publishers use computer software to format and combine text, data, photographs, charts and other graphic art or illustrations into prototypes of pages and other documents that are to be printed. Desktop publishing is the use of a computer to create various graphic products for the use of advertising, personal and/or business. For example some of the products that may be created are business cards, stationary, newsletters, cards, invitations, etc. (8).

Educational Background

Although there is a lot of software out there that will allow you to create various graphical products, there are courses that you can take that will teach you to use some of the more advanced software applications. There are also degree and career diploma programs in graphic design and desktop publishing. You can attend schools at the community college level and university level. There are also advanced degree programs. There are some correspondence courses that are available at various schools that offer graphic design majors, and diploma programs in graphic design/artist and desktop publishing. However, according to the Bureau of Labor Statistics, there are generally no education requirements for the job of desktop publishers (8). Many of the software programs that are available are pretty easy to learn, but you have to have the patience to turn out quality work. Sometimes, people don't have the time to sit down and thumb through a lot of different items and graphics to select one that will represent what they may want to express.

Areas of Desktop Publishing

Two specific areas are desktop publishing and graphic design. According to the Merriam Webster Dictionary, desktop publishing is the production of printed matter by the means of desktop computer having a layout program that integrates text and graphics. Graphic design is the art or profession of using design elements (such as typography or images) to convey information or create an affect; also includes products of this art.

Completing My Desktop Publishing Courses

I have worked with various computer software programs that have allowed me to create graphics. There are limited graphic features in some of the word processing and graphic programs, such as MS Word and PowerPoint. You can also do some graphics in MS Excel and MS Access. I wanted to start a personalized greeting card business, but I haven't completed a course per se. I have created cards for my mom, which added a personal touch, because the cards included the person's name.

Creating Opportunities in Desktop Publishing

One fascinating idea that has come about with the desktop publishing is creating greeting cards. I don't know if you have gone to the store and didn't find a greeting card that said exactly what you wanted to say. Being able to create a personalized greeting card with an individual's name, or even a portrait in pencil or paint, is an exciting new approach to personalizing greeting cards. Store bought cards are lovely and convenient, especially for those who like reading and picking out cards for various occasions. However, being one to add personalized touches to a card can be lucrative to the person who has the skills to convey what a customer is requesting for their specific cards.

What is so Cool About This Opportunity?

People need cards everyday for various occasions. Most stores only carry cards for the more popular occasions. The occasions that are unique will require that a card be made. Sometimes, one card doesn't say everything that you want to say. An individual can buy two cards or have one card that says everything that they need to say. Sometimes, you will be able to add other personal touches, such as a painting or drawing of the individual. If you have drawing or painting skills, or know of someone that you could hire for cheap, this could be a very lucrative venture in personalized cards.

There are so many different opportunities if you have a computer, a good printer and graphical software. For example, you can assist someone in making stationary for various occasions. You can do wedding invitations, birthday invitations, business cards, etc.

How Could You Go About Starting This Opportunity?

The first thing you will have to do is decide what type of work that you want to do. You can do either greeting cards, general stationary or both. With the greeting cards, you should begin by putting together a selection of cards in a portfolio with various sayings. If you want to start out on a budget, you could do a portfolio showing the next holiday coming up. In addition to that, you will need to do some for general occasions, such as birthday, get well soon, as well as other that don't happen on a specific day of the year.

Once you have put together a good portfolio, you can begin posting flyers or sending out brochures of your services. It would be a good idea to have in addition to finished cards, some general sayings for various occasions that may not be in a specific card. People will have the choice of choosing a saying and placing it in the card they desire.

You can do a variety of things to advertise. For one, you can host a party with a showing of your cards. If you live in a neighborhood or an apartment complex, you can easily go door to door with a flyer mentioning that you have a portfolio that can be seen by appointment. If you can afford to make catalogs, that can also be a good marketing tool. If you can afford to leave more than one flyer with a house, especially if you speak to the individual that lives in the house, this could be cheap labor in that they can distribute some flyers to friends, etc. It would be ideal to leave two or three extra flyers with each household.

Make sure you account for turnaround time upon receipt of payment. It is important to be efficient and diligent when processing orders. Some people may have last minute jobs for you to do, but if you sincerely can't do it, it is best to let them know. Advertising that people should give you so much time when processing orders is important so that it cuts down on the number of last minute orders. If people know that you have a two-week turn-around time, this keeps them from making impossible demands. If they have a need to have a job done, they will process their orders ahead of schedule.

Once you are done with the order, you should promptly deliver the order to the customer. It is important that you consider delivery time and other factors when processing orders. If you are advertising over the Internet, you will have to take into consideration mail time, processing time, and check clearing time. If you can accept debit or credit cards, these orders process a lot quicker than accepting checks.

You can always hire additional people if the load gets to be too much. Never try to do everything yourself if there is more than you can handle. It is easier to hire someone to help you, when the orders are overwhelming than to turn away customers who are requesting your services.

Using quality materials is very important. It's easy to find cheap materials that are not of good quality. It is important to have returning customers. One customer can use you at least 10 occasions, such as Christmas, New Year's Day, birthdays, Valentine's Day, Easter, Anniversary's, etc. For example, I have never seen a card in the store for Elder's' Day, which it may be available in some places. I began to accumulate supplies and software to make cards, and when my mother needed cards for various occasions, I was able to make these cards for her. The unique twist of making these cards for her is that I was able to put the individual's name on the card, which added a very personalized touch. She pretty much wrote what she wanted to say on each card making it her own. Instead of her signing the card with her signature, I personalized it with her name in a very fancy font. The card was simply beautiful and very personal. In addition to an Elder's Day card, I also made her two birthday cards.

You could also start a subscription card service. You can have clients that pay a monthly fee for a package of cards. What you will do is maintain a calendar for the cards, where the individual can pick out cards for various occasions. This person can rest assured that the cards will be delivered without them having to remind themselves just before the date. You will maintain a calendar of dates and where to mail the card and from whom. This is a great way to have a steady stream of monthly income coming in.

As with the greeting card business, you can also do stationary. Stationary can be for people who write personal letters or for business purposes. Some people need business cards, whether they own a business or just a personal way to give someone their information. There are just so many useful things where stationary can be used. Small businesses may not need as much as a large corporation. If you can offer then reasonable prices, you can have a new found customer.

Sometimes, people may have a newsletter that they want to publish. This can actually be a huge order, depending on the number of people that reads this newsletter. You can publish the newsletter electronically and send it to every customer, or you can print it out and either distributes the newsletter or the customer can distribute it. There are just so many things that you can get involved with in a desktop publishing business.

FASHION

What is Fashion?

Fashion, according to the Merriam-Webster Dictionary, can be defined as "a prevailing custom, usage, or style; the prevailing style (as in dress) during a particular time; a garment in such a style always wears the latest. According to the Bureau of Labor Statistics, "clothing designers create and help produce men's, women's, children's apparel, including casual wear, suits, sportswear, formalwear, outerwear, maternity, and intimate apparel (9)."

Educational Background of Fashion Careers

Some people who work in the fashion industry, such as fashion designer or fashion merchandiser, usually holds a bachelor's degree. Also, there are many fashion design programs that offer up to a master's degree in fashion design or fashion merchandising. In addition, there are the traditional schools, where you receive classroom training, or you can attend an online school to work on your degree in fashion. When earning a master's degree in fashion, you have the opportunity to go into teaching. I completed a fashion design and merchandising diploma course through a correspondence school, as well as a diploma course in dressmaking and design. While some designers receive formal training, there are some designers are even self-taught. According to the Bureau of Labor Statistics, The National Association of Schools of Art and Design accredits approximately 300 postsecondary institutions with programs in art and design (9).

Areas in Fashion

Two of the most visible areas of fashion are fashion design and fashion merchandising. Also, there is accessories design; textile design, jewelry design, buyer, and foot wear design, within the fashion industry. As a fashion designer, you will work on creating the next fashion trend. It requires you to come up with fashion for each season and to help promote that line, usually through a runway show and/or through a catalog sale, or store sale. Being a fashion designer can be very expensive, when you think of the entire process required to show a line. For one, you would have to create your line with enough pieces to carry a collection for that season. Once you have created the pieces you would need people to sew the garment. Once you have sewn the line, you will need models who can model the clothing for you. You will carry the expense of not only creating a line, but also mass producing this line and distributing it.

When creating a line, you have to think of the possible considerations. Fashion requires fabric and all the subsequent supplies that go into making that garment. You could do it yourself, but when it is time to mass produce the line to be distributed to many stores, one person could never get this done alone.

As an accessories designer, you will focus on the accessories that are used to complement the fashion. Accessories may comprise of handbags, belts, scarves, or ties. These items are used to enhance your fashion and accentuate its style.

A textile designer works with the actual fabric. As a textile designer, you may be responsible for creating fabric to make clothing from various materials that are natural or manmade. In addition, you may be responsible for putting a unique design on that fabric, which gives the garment a 2-D or 3-D effect.

Jewelry designers works with creating jewelry. As a jewelry designer, you will make various pieces of jewelry, such as necklaces, bracelets, earrings, brooches, rings, etc. These pieces can accentuate the total outfit and make it look elegant and sleek, or play it down to make it cool and casual.

A buyer usually works for a retail outfit and is responsible for purchasing clothing for a store. It is important as a buyer to know trends and buy things that the consumer will have an interest. This is a tough job, because you have to predict what is hot and what is not.

You can buy many items that seem like they will be appealing, but they could sit on racks for a long time.

Finally a footwear designer designs various types of shoes. There are many types of footwear from casual and athletic to elegant shoes. Shoes are one of those accessories that you need for all types of occasions. For example, there are work shoes/boots; athletic for exercise, sports, and dance. Also, there are dressy heels for formal occasions, as well as casual shoes for just walking around.

Completing My Fashion Courses

I can tell you that I have always had a burning passion to go to fashion design school. While I was in high school, I subscribed to every fashion magazine that I could afford. I would comb through these magazines to see the latest fashion trend. I have requested catalogs from various fashion schools around the country. The unfortunate thing was that back then; there wasn't any financial aid to attend the schools I had an interest. If you didn't have the money to pay for these schools, you were pretty much out of luck. Today, financial aid is available to attend many schools for fashion. Although I have traveled down a different path, I have always come back to fashion. Because of my inability to pay for school, I enrolled and completed a correspondence course in fashion merchandising and design, and dressmaking and design. These were great courses in that it gave me a great understanding of the fashion industry, and great sewing skills. It really helped me to decide if fashion design was something that I would really want to pursue.

Creating Opportunities in Fashion

One unique opportunity that isn't widely publicized is creating fashion for disabled people. People with limbs missing can have customized clothing that will fit their needs and lifestyles. Most fashion that is created is for the average person, and someone with a limb missing may not be as mobile as an individual that is able to walk. Sometimes, adjustments need to be made in order to accommodate that individual's position, whether in a wheel chair or walking with a walker.

What is so Cool About This Opportunity?

The unique thing about creating clothes for individuals with disabilities is that it is a unique opportunity to help someone who may not be able to find clothes for themselves to look as stylish as anyone else.

There may be one or two companies that actually service this market, but for the most part, people that are interested in fashion are interested in the average consumer.

How Could You Go About Starting This Opportunity?

If you don't already know how to design and/or sew, you can take the opportunity to either complete a degree program (associates, bachelors, or masters degrees) in fashion design or you may choose to take a correspondence course or career diploma. You would have to assess what exactly do you know and how much you need to learn to enter this market. Although correspondence courses give you a great deal of information about fashion merchandising and design, to get further and seek greater knowledge, you will probably need to take additional courses in order to get a full understanding of the fashion design or fashion merchandising process.

Once you have taken courses and have decided that you want to enter into this unique opportunity, you will have to gather together materials, and find ways of obtaining a mailing list of these individuals. Because this is such a small market, I would suggest making your company national and/or global because access just people in your location may not be a large client list. You can use avenues, such as the Internet to advertise your services.

You can get patterns on an as needed basis. You could gather together the supplies that you will need, such as buttons, fabric, some sample patterns, notions, etc. You can make a few sample items to show people the quality and skill of your work. It would be a great idea to do a variety of garments, such as a dress, pants, skirt, jacket (lined), shirt, etc. This gives you the opportunity to showcase your skills in a variety of garments. Start a portfolio of all garments sewn. It would be a good idea if you had a model, but if you don't you can make your own model. I've personally taken some foam board and made moveable legs and arms, with a torso and pinned them together to make a model.

Because it has moveable joints, you can use it for the average person, or you can remove a part as needed to emphasize an individual that may be missing a limb. When you take pictures, take pictures of the front and back.

Once you have your sample garments, you can construct a website, but you can also advertise on some of the popular sites where you are able to sell your garments. Make sure you take high quality pictures. If you aren't able to take excellent quality pictures, you may want to hire a professional photographer to do it.

Next, you should advertise your business in as many ways as possible, sticking to your budget. You can use many social networking sites or some other venue to spread the word. In addition, you may want to have some business cards printed, some flyers and brochures that explain what you do.

You will need to give yourself some time to sew and deliver the items. It is probably best to calculate how long it takes to do each item; how long do you plan on spending per day in creating garments?; What would be a realistic turn around for an individual that has ordered a garment from you?

Always be diligent in processing any order from a customer. You want to create high quality items, but at the same time, you want to be fast and efficient. The worst thing you can do is to take an order and not be able to deliver. Be realistic in what you are able to do and what you are willing to do?

Think about the method of delivery. There are various ways that you can send these items. Check into the various companies that deliver and make sure that you have more than one on hand, in case there are problems with one delivery service.

REAL ESTATE

What is Real Estate?

Real estate is property in building and land. These buildings can be commercial or residential. Commercial real estate is very different from residential in that it doesn't require as much capital as in residential real estate, and there are many more vacancies. Real estate can involve selling and/or buying of personal property to an individual. With real estate investment, it involves the buying and selling of real estate, but more for profit (14).

Educational Background

Real estate is one field that you can take a short real estate course to become a licensed real estate salesperson. There are some advanced degrees in real estate. According to the BLS, an individual who sells and buys property is required to obtain a state license.

A bachelor's degree in real estate helps prepare an individual in appraisal, sales and brokerage, property management, and mortgage lending. It gives an individual a well rounded education in that it is usually found in the business school, and with liberal arts requirements.

The curriculum helps individuals understand real estate market analysis, site selection, investment analysis, economics, and professional service that support a real estate transaction.

A real estate student can expect to study accounting, personnel management, finance, information systems, management and marketing.

To be successful in real estate, you must possess the right personality. You must be mature, trustworthy, and enthusiastic about the field.

Some of the career paths in real estate are appraisal, escrow, mortgage finance, residential practices, real estate law, brokerage, real property management, real estate insurance, etc.

Obtaining a master's degree in real estate can lead to a career in real estate agencies, consulting, corporate and residential development, and mortgage brokerage and property management. A curriculum might include contract management, customer relationship management, and project management according to the curriculum at New England College (24).

There are even several schools that offer a PhD in real estate. A PhD program in real estate prepares graduates in real estate, capital markets, housing and urban economics. It prepares individuals for academic positions in real estate and finance, and technical research positions in the industry. These programs can prepare students to deal with issues such as structured financing, contract design and pricing, regulatory issues in real estate finance, real estate cycles, real options, agglomeration economies and the structure and operation of mortgage, housing and land markets according to the curriculum at University of California, Berkeley (23).

Areas of Real Estate

Some people may get involved in real estate sales, and there is also real estate investment. Real estate investment can be an exciting career in that an individual purchases properties and sell them for a profit. Some people get properties, renovate them, then turn them around and make a profit.

Another area of real estate that is relatively new is green building using natural products of the land to make homes. Some homes include cob homes, log homes, straw bale homes, etc.

Completing My Real Estate Courses

Real estate investment was a field that I had strong aspirations and wanted to get involved. I personally like the idea of taking something that is completely or partially ruined, building it up and beautifying it into something fabulous. I had a strong desire to be involved in real estate investment with fixer-uppers. I had enrolled in a course when I was 18 years old that taught real estate investment, but it was so advanced, that I wound up giving it away. This is definitely one area that I would have loved to get heavily involved, but I just was never able to stabilize myself to commit to it.

Creating Opportunities in Real Estate

I have always had dreams of having my own home, and when my career suffered serious setbacks, I was ready to do anything by all means to own my dream home. I wanted to combine a way of working at the same time, because I was experiencing long bouts of unemployment, which is what led me to write this book.

The idea that I came up with was to build a green home using materials from the Earth, and starting a farm with a small store, where I would sell fruits, vegetables, homemade candles, homemade soaps, clothing, etc. There are several videos on the Internet of people, including women, who have documented their home building venture. I became intrigued that women would actually take the time to build their own home. The women in some videos began doing all of the work themselves, then eventually got help along the way. Some had maintained a full-time job while they worked on their homes part-time. In addition to that particular opportunity, you could start a green construction company, where you can build these homes for other people.

What is so Cool About This Opportunity?

With today's economy and it being so hard to secure loans, using green material is a very cheap alternative to traditional home building. It can be a fun family affair, which is cheap labor, in building your dream home, but more importantly, if you decide to start a green construction company, you can use your family as labor in addition to the family that you are building the home for as labor too. It could be a wonderful way to earn a living, as it will help build a home for a family.

One particular home that I was interested in was the cob home. This home is made from dirt, clay and water, where you have to find the right texture for the soil that you are using. Be advised that these homes cannot be built everywhere. You must test the soil and get together batches of soil to find the mixture that will make a sturdy brick for your home. Once you have found the right mixture for your climate, then you will begin the process of making this mixture and drying the bricks.

The great thing about these homes is that they are very sturdy, and even through rain storms, they last a lifetime. These homes are very popular in Europe and are becoming popular in the United States.

There are several other homes that you can build that may take less time than the cob home, but are a little more expensive. For example, there are straw bale homes, log homes, and adobe homes. Each of the homes may cost a little more to build, because you have to buy a certain straw bale in order to make the home. Log homes can be purchase pre cut.

With the straw bale homes, they are made from rectangle bales of hay that are stacked up. There are several books out there that will guide you step-by-step on how to build these types of homes.

How Could You Go About Starting This Opportunity?

The first thing you should do is to invest in several books that will guide you in the process. For one, I would buy a book that teaches you how to build several types of green homes. I would also invest in a good book on frame structure, wiring and plumbing, unless you want to find someone who can professionally do these jobs. Ultimately, you will have the house inspected to make sure that it meets all building codes. I would read each book from front to back at least once to understand the general concept of what is expected. Any words that you don't understand you should have a dictionary available so that you will understand the lingo of the book. It may be a good idea, if you have your family assisting you, that you all read the book so that each one of you can understand the entire process.

When involving yourself in a typical real estate transaction (assisting a consumer in purchasing or selling a home), it is recommended that you set up a real estate team. This would include an attorney, accountant, insurance agent, financing resources, property resources, and contractors/repair people (14). Although this is ideal for typical homes, with green homes, if this is within your financial reach, it should be considered. If you can't do it immediately, ultimately when you start to make money, this should definitely be on your list of things to do. It would save you a lot of heartache, because you will be within your legal realm. You will also avoid any financial pitfalls, with taxes, bookkeeping, etc.

Start researching where to purchase the various materials that are necessary for building the home. It would be a good idea to keep a list of various suppliers, so when one supplier doesn't have enough material or is out of a particular material, you will be able to go to another supplier. Know exactly where you will go to purchase all the materials that you will need.

If you can find property cheap, begin by practicing with your own home. The more you do it, the more you will become skilled at it, and your home will be an example of what other homes will look like. This actually gives people the opportunity to see your home, and know exactly what they are getting.

Once you have perfected your own home, you can begin to advertise your services. Going through the process with your own home will let you know if this is something that you truly want to do. In any event, you will have your own home that you could live in, rent or sell. Currently, these homes don't have any resale value. They may not be financed by a mortgage, so you may have to provide some type of payment plan, or you can rent these homes out to individuals.

You may question whether to do a lease/purchase option or outright sell option. According to the book, "Buy Low, Rent Smart, Sell High: Real Estate Investing for the Long Run," it is recommended that the lease/purchase option would create a win-win situation, but as an investor, you should be open to an outright sell option, if a buyer wants to purchase a home (17).

You can begin to advertise your company in the area that you plan on building. You can find various properties on the Internet, where you may be able to purchase land cheap. If you want, you can either pre-purchase the land or you can have a list of properties available that you can tell individuals, who want to build a home, and they can make the arrangement to purchase the land on their own.

People may be skeptical at first. Sometimes, it takes awhile for people to catch on to things, so your home will be the model that you will show them to sell them on the idea. If you involve another family, whose home you are building, you may want to offer them a substantial discount, since they are helping to build their own home. Finding efficient and cost effective ways of building these homes, you could make substantially more money, because you and/or your family or laborers are the ones that are involved with the building process.

HEALTHCARE

What is a physician?

A physician is an individual who has credentials that certifies him or her as a doctor or MD and is qualified to practice medicine. This individual has gone to college, medical school, and depending on his or her specialty has done a residency in their specialty field. He or she performs health diagnosis according to his or her specialty and prescribes a treatment plan.

Educational Background

A person who wants to become a physician trains for a minimum of eight years in post secondary education. An individual takes various science courses that are required by the medical school. This individual will also take the MCAT (Medical College Admission Test) in addition to applying to medical school. If the individual is accepted into medical school, he or she will spend the next four years taking the required courses to become an MD. Once he or she is done with medical school there is a residency requirement according to the specialty that the doctor has an interest. For example, there are residencies for surgery, pediatrics, obstetrics and gynecology, plastic surgery, dermatology, etc. Each specialty varies in the number of years in residency that the doctor has to do.

Areas of Medicine

Although there are many areas of medicine, focus will only be made on the areas that pertain to the weekend primary care clinics. The clinic would only consist of primary care needs, such as pediatrics, family practice, internal medicine, obstetrics and gynecology, dentistry, and optometry. The purpose of focusing on only primary care is to have the basic medical needs met for each potential patient.

Pediatrics is the field of medicine that deals with patients that are under the age of 18. A doctor in this field addresses the medical needs of children, and once they become of age, they would go on to see either a family practitioner or internal medicine, or in the case of a female, she would see a gynecologist. The residency requirements for a pediatrician are approximately 6 years long. Depending on your specialty, it could take longer.

Family practitioner is the field of medicine that deals with general practice medicine. This individual can see an entire family, children and adults. The residency requirement to become a family practitioner is three years. Once you have completed medical school, residency requirements and pass the licensing boards, you are eligible to carry the title Medical Doctor (MD).

Internal medicine is the field of medicine that deals with the entire patient medically as opposed to surgically. According to the Enclopaedia Britannica, internal medicine deals with the entire patient, and not just an organ system covering diagnosis and medical, rather surgical treatments. The residency requirement for internal medicine may take up to six years, depending on the specialty that one wants.

Preparing for Medical School

Although I never made it to medical school, I was able to sample a little about what the healthcare field is like. My experience is not in the capacity of interacting with patients, but more on the administrative side of healthcare, taking a course in medical claims and billing, and medical transcription. Medical school would have been a long haul for me. Although I do have a graduate degree, I would have been require to take the MCAT, return to school and take the prerequisites, that would have taken me approximately 1 year to complete. Then if accepted into medical school, it would have taken 4 years. My area of interest was pediatrics, which I assumed the residency requirements was between 1½ to 3 years. However, after completing my research, I found out that the requirements could be as much as 6 years. In total, it would have taken me as much as 11 years to complete all the educational requirements. This is okay, when you are in your twenties, and maybe you have reached certain goals that you had set out to achieve. But, when you are in your later years, and you find that you haven't achieved the goals that you wanted to in your personal life, you have to sometimes take inventory as to what is most important in your own life. It was a great plan that had this been an idea in my younger days, I would have been happy to pursue this challenge, but unfortunately there is so much that I haven't achieved that I had to reprioritize my goals and try to be more realistic in doing things to accomplish my personal passions.

The Alternative to Medical School—Physician Assistant

When I saw that the length of time was an issue in attending medical school, I thought about another field choice, physician assistant. Physician assistants perform similar duties as a medical doctor, however, they are under the guidance of a physician and also, they are sometimes not authorized to prescribe medication.

The time to complete a physician assistant program can be between 3 to 5 years. The physician assistant program can be completed at the undergraduate level where a bachelor's degree is issued. However, physician assistants usually go on to obtain a master's degree, which is becoming the standard.

Initially, I wanted to attend physician assistant school. At some schools, they offer a Master's program, where you could explore this option provided that you completed certain requirements, such as science classes, and work experience. If you have an undergraduate degree in another field, it would be a matter of taking the science requirements and meeting certain work requirements in order to apply to the program.

If you are someone who can afford to give a few hours on the weekend, without losing the shirt off your back, then volunteering, especially in healthcare, can be very beneficial to those who receive your services.

The healthcare industry is one of the few fields that will always need people. People are always getting sick for one reason or another. There is a great opportunity available for an individual or individuals, who may have a background in a healthcare field or may be willing to go to school.

Areas of Physician Assistant

The medical areas of physician assistant pretty much run along the same areas that are available as a physician. Becoming a physician assistant doesn't require you to do a residency, as is required when you are becoming a doctor.

Creating an Opportunity in Volunteering/Healthcare

One creative idea is as a physician or physician assistant, where you can create a weekend employment opportunity to help the uninsured and the underinsured, that could also serve as a volunteer opportunity. I'm sure that you have been keeping up with the current events of today, and realize that lack of insurance has been an issue for a long time with individuals who are employed. Many Americans are faced with not being properly insured.

A physician or a physician assistant could gain valuable exposure, so the lack of employment opportunity is not a problem in these fields, unlike other fields. Being able to establish some way to do volunteer work, would be a great way to help others and still be able to earn a living.

I was working at a large retail store, and decided that I may want to get into the healthcare field. I had planned on going to school to become a physician scientist, which with a bachelor degree would be an approximate 8 year stint. It was four years of medical school and approximately four years to complete your PhD in research. Unfortunately, things didn't work out financially, and after doing more research, I realize that although I had good intentions, it didn't become a field that I was truly excited about. I was however excited about the plan to create these weekend clinics that would serve the uninsured and the underinsured, and allow them to go to the doctor for free.

The idea for physician assistant came about, because when I was unable to attend medical school due to financial reasons, I saw physician assistant as an alternative. I wanted to be able to achieve this dream, yet at the same time be able to start a family—get married and have children.

With a weekend clinic, a physician or physician assistant could schedule primary care services, so that an individual with limited or no healthcare coverage can go to the doctor and be treated.

This practice on the weekend doesn't interfere with your own practice or job, unless you work weekends. Being able to give a few hours of your time to help those who are less fortunate can be a very rewarding experience.

The primary care clinic would consist of a doctor for each of the following fields, pediatrics, obstetrics and gynecology, family practice, dentistry, optometry, and internal medicine. What these doctors would do is see patients for general check-ups on the weekend. Depending on the workload, it may be only a few patients for a few hours. Any serious ailments that can't be treated at that time, that patient would be referred to a doctor outside of the clinic. It could be another primary care physician or a specialist. This is just a way to get people who are uninsured or underinsured the quality of healthcare that is necessary without the doctor losing the shirt off of his or her back.

It is hopeful that these clinics can operate in areas, where they are truly needed, and that it would be beneficial in helping those who are in need of medical treatment and screenings but can't afford it or don't have adequate insurance to go to the doctor.

A patient would have their initial consultations at the clinic. If there was anything wrong, they would get a second opinion, if they felt that it is necessary. The second opinion would come from a doctor outside of the clinic. Once that doctor's second opinion came back, the patient would either schedule to have this ailment treated and/or be seen by a specialist.

In addition to having the opportunity to see a specialist, if the patient needs to go to the emergency room, that patient would be allowed to go without seeking prior permission.

Each patient would go through an orientation, where he or she would receive training on how the clinic operates, and also about the different primary care physicians and their roles. They would also receive training about making appointments, everything they need to know to function at the clinic. Once they had completed the orientation, each patient would receive an identification card with their picture, which acts as an insurance card. Whenever that patient needed to go for a second opinion, a specialist, or to the emergency room, they would present the card, which contains billing information on the back, and that healthcare facility or doctor would send the clinic a bill, and we would process it and pay it.

There were various resources that could be considered in raising funds for the clinic. For one, I had come up with this idea of using change to help raise capital for transitional housing for homeless veterans a few years back. Change is one of the things that even in bad economic times, people don't always mind sparing. Even little children may drop a penny or two to help someone. The idea isn't to exploit children, but an idea that through small doses of donations, we could help the homeless, thus, the economically disadvantage that are uninsured or underinsured.

This pennies and dimes fundraiser works where a bank with a nationwide presence would be approached about placing large water jugs with advertising on it to raise funds for the clinic. The jug would be placed in the bank and customers, as well as employees could donate coins, pennies or dimes and place them in the jugs. Nickels and quarters would be welcomed and place them in the jug, too. The idea behind the nickel and dime was the campaign slogan that was used, and I was able to find a catchy slogan that rhymed with using dimes and pennies, which is why the idea of using dimes and pennies had come about. At the end of the day, each jug at each location would be deposited at the bank.

The bookkeeper or administrative assistant's role would be to ensure that the jugs of coins are deposited. If the bank teller or other bank employee agreed to deposit the money, the bookkeeper or administrative assistant would just go online and check the daily deposits everyday and record it in our accounting/bookkeeping records.

In addition to the pennies and dimes fundraiser, we would also do other fund raisers. Some things that could be considered are fashion shows, art shows, bake sales, etc. There could also be various online solicitations for donations and letter sent to various individuals or companies for donations.

Based on the amount of money that can be raised, would be a determinant as to whether free services could be offered. The goal was to raise enough funds to sustain the clinic and expand in other areas where a clinic of this kind would be needed. Although this idea isn't exactly innovative in itself, it is however unique in the way it raises funds and allows individuals to go to the clinic for free. If there weren't enough funds to allow people to receive free treatment, we would charge a small co-payment.

My primary job during the week would have been research and my weekend duties would have been pediatrics at the clinic. I enjoy being around children, and have always longed to have my own.

The way that buildings would have been obtained would be through government resources. Sometimes, buildings are closed down for various reasons, and sold for auction, as well as medical equipment. Sometimes offices move into larger or smaller facilities, or they upgrade their offices for their convenience. In addition, medical equipment usually becomes obsolete, and is auctioned off. The plan was to try to purchase some of those buildings and equipment in order to run the clinic. Although the equipment would not be as advanced as the equipment that may be in current use, it is still functional. Using recycled equipment wouldn't diminish the quality of service that each patient would receive. This is why the clinic would have made it optional for an individual to receive a second opinion to raise their confidence level that the care that they are receiving is the same quality of care they would receive had they visited a regular doctor's office. The building and equipments would have cut down the cost of having to build a facility or purchase expensive equipment. However, It would have been a challenge trying to find a building that has been vacated in a place where there is a dire need for a clinic, so there would have had to been alternatives to finding buildings or possibly constructing a new building. But, the government would have been the primary source for finding buildings and medical equipment to start a clinic.

If it becomes a challenge trying to see patients on a weekend basis, perhaps one might consider a few evenings during the week and maybe adding additional primary care physicians.

If physicians or physician assistants could donate a few hours around their schedules, this could be beneficial towards those who may not have adequate insurance. Depending on the needs of the city or town, a physician/physician assistant may only donate two to three hours on the weekend to see patients.

What is so Cool About This Opportunity?

This opportunity is so cool because it is an opportunity to be a part of something huge in resolving the healthcare issue.

If we are able to increase consumer confidence in health care, we could increase the number of people, who will have the confidence to go to the doctor and feel that the doctor is doing everything that he can do to take care of his or her well being.

This is where the orientation to the clinic could be beneficial. The orientation, just prior to an individual receiving their card, will be introducing the potential patients to various areas that are operative inside the clinic, as well as, several specialties.

How Could You Go About Starting This Opportunity?

The first thing you would do is really try to assess whether there is a healthcare crisis in the area that you have an interest. If there isn't a need for a clinic and other government facilities are in operation, you will really be wasting your time.

This type of business entity would be a non-profit organization, which would have to be a corporation in order to be eligible. A non-profit organization is not required to pay taxes and has various tax advantages.

If you are not hiring a lawyer to take care all of the necessary business start-up, etc, you will have to determine various factors. You will have to come up with a fictitious name to identify the organization. Once you have made a determination of what type of business, you can begin to purchase all of the supplies and equipment that will be used to run your business.

You will have to develop a relationship with locals, banks, who can be key players in helping out. You will need people to handle the administrative tasks, as well as other non-medical tasks.

You can check the governments' website to find out about auctions and/or sales of buildings and equipment. This will be the greatest challenge finding buildings, so you may have to wind up building a facility. To find out if there are any buildings available through the government, you can go to the USA.gov website, which will give you a list of buildings available by state. Also, for medical equipment, the website lists the type of equipment that is up for auction. This website can be a valuable resource for not only medical equipment, but also for medical supplies, furniture, etc.

Now that you know what type of entity, non-profit corporation, a building and a name, you will want to start with fundraisers and building renovations. You have the building and medical equipment, so you will need to have it renovated to hospital standards. In addition, it won't hurt to start having fundraisers to get the cash flowing. You will be spending quite a bit of time just getting together the foundation of your clinic, prior to its opening its doors.

There may be laws and regulations that you have to follow pertaining to opening a clinic. It would be in your best interest to either consult with a lawyer or find out about any legal requirements to starting a clinic of this sort. It may be beneficial to consult with a lawyer who will be able to set up all the start-up and corporate paperwork in order to establish that you are starting a clinic. But, if there are budget constraints, you can visit a bookstore or library and find out if there are books available to start a non-profit corporation, and the requirements.

Your building is being renovated, and you are starting to solicit a nationwide bank to find out if you can run your pennies and dime campaign to raise funds. The reason why you look for a bank with a nationwide presence is that if your future goal is to build a network of clinics nationwide, you will be dealing with one bank, instead of dealing with several different banks. The accounting is much simpler to have to access one account online and record the deposits for the day, instead of having to access several different banks. It is possible, but more feasible to work with one bank. If you know that your intentions are only to deal within a certain region, then by all means you can use a local bank.

Your facility is renovated and you have raised some funds to help supplement your patients' healthcare. You should have been advertising the opening of the clinic, so there is huge anticipation that this will be the place that people will use for their primary medical needs. The next step will be to organizing your first orientation, which introduces your new patients to the clinic. When I was in college, I took a public health course, which stated that you can put as many clinics in a community, but if you don't educate the people the importance of getting their health needs met, having the clinic wouldn't do any good to the community. This is where the idea came about to have an orientation that would require everyone, male and female, to listen to all physicians at the clinic. A male patient would be required to know about obstetrics and gynecology, even though he would never see this type of doctor. The concept of the clinic is really about education.

His knowledge of obstetrics and gynecology may never be of use to him, but if he were married, it may be something where he might be able to pass on to his significant other, a female family member or acquaintance. The entire concept of the orientation at the clinic is really about educating each patient about the importance of receiving medical treatment.

The continual raising of funds is crucial. It is better to have a surplus of funds in the event of an emergency, than to raise funds and think that that is more than enough. Patients can get sick with serious ailments, and because the facility is a primary care facility, you will only be able to do so much. A cancer patient will probably need chemotherapy. This individual would need to go to an oncologist in order to be treated. This can cost some serious money.

There are other books that you may need to reference in order to start up and run a successful clinic. There are probably some government resources that would be beneficial. You should be a person that researches and gain as much knowledge as possible in order to run a successful clinic. In addition, if you are someone who is not good with writing grant proposals, you can either get a book or hire someone who can write your grant proposal.

This clinic is beneficial in a lot of ways. For one, you are helping individuals who are either uninsured or underinsured, and you are also creating employment opportunities. If in the beginning you are unable to secure enough funds to hire someone, there are several options that you can take in order to secure help. You can seek volunteers. This looks great on their resume for their own future employment prospects, especially someone who has been out of work a long time. If they aren't in dire need of money, this could be a good way for this person to gain valuable medical office experience. Then there are individuals who can afford to volunteer and it is just a way to keep busy.

Also, if you feel compelled to compensate someone, you can go through AmeriCorps, which is a volunteer opportunity where an individual can earn compensation, plus some educational benefits. Currently, the maximum that an individual can work under this plan is five years, so if you don't mind switching up people for various positions, every five years, it is a valuable way for an individual to gain work experience, with some pretty cool benefits. Also the individual is not required to return after the first year of service.

Organizing different events can be done by an event planner. There are so many things to do to raise money. My plan was to have fashion shows and art exhibits where artwork can be auctioned off. Also, there are bake sales.

Another idea is that if you acquire a building and do not use the entire space, you could rent office space to other businesses. What a great way to help a cause by renting a space and knowing that it is going to help people who otherwise couldn't afford health insurance.

Your first clinic could start out as your pilot clinic and once the kinks are smoothed out, you can start clinics in other areas wherever it is necessary. Some clinics won't be successful, some will be. Hopefully, the clinic will maintain good books in that they will realize which clinics will not be feasible.

CLEANING SERVICE

What is a Cleaning Service?

I realize that with the presentation of these chapters that some definitions are really self-explanatory, such as this current chapter being presented. A cleaning service, you may wonder, "why do I need to define it? Although the definition may be obvious, it is important to understand the inner workings of any career field, as well as a cleaning service. Your traditional cleaning service consists of the use of cleaning supplies, broom, mop, vacuum, cleaning chemicals, etc. These items will allow you to perform cleaning functions in order to make a house or a commercial area bacteria and germ free. This particular business is particularly my favorite one because as a youngster, I spent a lot of time dreaming about my own home. Growing up, I would thumb through a Spiegels or Sears catalog which was filled with furniture, appliances and clothing. I would dream about my home picking out furniture, appliances, curtains, and children's furniture. Our house was crowded, so you could imagine that I wanted to declare my freedom as soon as possible. I always vowed that I would meet the man of my dreams, we would buy a house and my children would have their own room. When you visit homes of others and you see how immaculate and finely decorated their home looks, you could only fantasize that you will grow up to have a home that looks like theirs.

According to a dictionary, to define cleaning service (or clean) is to provide assistance in a home or commercial business to free a place or area, from dirt, marks, or stains.

Educational Background

For a cleaning service, I haven't seen any educational requirements on the vocational or college levels. Cleaning is something that has been in existence throughout history. It is mainly taught at home from childhood, where you may have had responsibilities of cleaning the dishes, your room, or throwing out the trash. Traditionally, it was the mother or females that were responsible for cleaning of the home, if she didn't work outside the home. As a child, I remember receiving an allowance of five dollars a week to clean the dishes every day. Although as a child, I did try to do a lot more cleaning than was necessary, you grow up and realize the importance of cleaning.

Areas of Cleaning Service

People, who work outside of the home, don't always have the time or make the time to clean their own homes. In addition, in a business environment, a company usually hires a cleaning service to clean their office spaces. The two most common areas of cleaning are residential and commercial. For residential cleaning, it is mainly going into someone's home and providing a cleaning service, such as mopping, sweeping, vacuuming, cleaning the upholstery, walls, windows, bathroom, etc. In a commercial environment, you may provide cleaning by vacuuming, sweeping, buffing the floors, cleaning the windows, bathrooms, break room, conference rooms, etc. More than likely in a commercial setting, you would not be involved with cleaning an individual's personal desk space, but possibly throwing out their trash.

What I Have Learned About Cleaning?

I have observed single parents, who worked every day and gave the responsibility to their children to clean the home and prepare meals, which really showed me that cleaning a home every day can be a huge chore for someone who works every day. Also, being in the military, we were required to clean every day. It's a full-time job in itself to have to clean, so imagine having to work eight hours a day, with overtime, and coming home to clean (and cook) everyday. This is where this can be a great opportunity for an individual who doesn't have the time to clean every day.

Throughout the years, I have become a connoisseur of cleaning, learning how to treat different stains and dirt. In the past, my favorite cleaning products were products that are antibacterial, which cleans 99.9% of the known viruses and bacteria, to include HIV and herpes simplex viruses. But the one thing about cleaning products is that if you have small children around and these products are not secure, they can be potentially fatal to a child that may have access to those products. In recent years, many companies who are going green, have come out with products that are eco-friendly, biodegradable, and non-toxic. So, you may be asking yourself, what product could I use that would be safe for the environment and your children?

Creating Opportunities in Cleaning Service

When you think of the traditional way of cleaning, you would need different cleaners for furniture, floor, carpet, windows and glass, bathroom, upholstery, etc. What if you were able to eliminate most of these items, and replace it with one gadget with multiple attachments?

Running a professional steam cleaning service is a new twist on running a cleaning service. You require less equipment and the cleaning is safe for children and pets. Now in order to not slight cleaning services or the products that are used, you can create a steam cleaning service that is offered in addition to a person's traditional cleaning. Steam cleaning can be the extra special cleaning treatment, if you feel that it might cause waves to traditional cleaning services. The products are already on the market, so it is just a matter of you implementing these products into the services that you would provide.

I have always had dreams of having my own home, and when my career suffered serious setbacks, I was ready to do anything by all means to own a home. I wanted to combine a way of working at the same time.

What is so Cool About This Opportunity?

This is a cool opportunity, because there are so many people who work every day, and are too tired after a long day to clean up their home. Sometimes, it may be a special function that someone wants to have, and may not feel up to cleaning up to make their place look good. Providing a steam cleaning service can be that "in addition to" or "instead of" service for people who can't clean their home every day or are too tired to clean at all. With a steam cleaning service, all you need is the equipment and water, and the steam is so powerful that it also kills bacteria and germs.

How Could You Go About Starting This Opportunity?

There are so many different steam cleaning supplies available in stores and on TV. If you are someone who can't afford to purchase your equipment outright, you can either start out with a basic steamer providing limited services, or you can catch one of the online or TV ads that advertise a payment plan or free home trial offer, where you may pay a small amount plus shipping. This is a great way to finance your start-up, especially if you don't have good credit. Sometimes, these products offer other products for free, so if you do some investigating, and figure out what services you want to supply, you will be able to not only get your product with a small payment plan, but also get additional equipment to provide additional services. The more services you can supply, the more money you can make.

Another consideration is area. If you don't have a vehicle, you are going to be limited to where you will be able to travel. It would be in your best interest to group areas in close proximity on the same day, so that you will be able to get from client-to-client, quickly and efficiently. Your overall, general area should be pretty close to your home base, which would make you clientele and business easier to manage.

You will probably need some flyers and other business stationary to advertise your business. It wouldn't hurt to have business cards and possibly some brochures. Thank you cards would provide an added touch. When handing out flyers, you should hand out at least two flyers, and encourage individuals if they know of any others, to please pass the extra flyers along.

Everyone likes a clean home, but not everyone likes to clean. Wouldn't it be a great service to be able to fill that need?

BIBLIOGRAPHY

1. _____. *Milady's Standard Textbook of Cosmetology*. Albany, NY. Milady Publishing Company, 2000: 657.
2. American Bar Association. "Standing Committee on Paralegals." *What is a Paralegal?* 2011, *http://www.americanbar.org/groups/paralegals.html*. [accessed October 28, 2011].
3. Brand, Paul. How to Repair Your Car. MBI Publishing Co. St. Paul, MN. 2006.
4. Bureau of Labor Statistics. "Artist and Related Workers." *Occupational Outlook Handbook*, 2010-2011 Edition. December 17, 2009. 301
5. Bureau of Labor Statistics. "Automotive Service Technicians and Mechanics." *Occupational Outlook Handbook*, 2010-2011 Edition. December 17, 2009. Retrieved on October 28, 2011 from http://www.bls.gov/oes/2011/may/oes493023.htm
6. Bureau of Labor Statistics. "Computer Support Specialists." *Occupational Outlook Handbook*, 2010-2011 Edition. December 17, 2009, *http://www.bls.gov/oco/ocos306.htm*. [accessed October 28, 2011]
7. Bureau of Labor Statistics. "Fitness Trainers and Aerobic Instructors." *Occupational Outlook Handbook*, 2010-2011 Edition, May 17, 2011, *http://www.bls.gov/oes/current/oes399031.htm*. [accessed October 28, 2011].
8. Bureau of Labor Statistics. "Management, Scientific, and Technical Consulting Services." *Occupational Outlook Handbook*, 2010-2011 Edition, *http://www.bls.gov/oco/ocos306.htm*. December 17, 2009. [accessed October 28, 2011]

9. Bureau of Labor Statistics. Broadcasting. Occupational Outlook Handbook, 2010-2011 Edition. December 17, 2009. Retrieved on October 28, 2011 from *http://www.bls.gov/oco/cg/cgs017.htm*.

10. Bureau of Labor Statistics. Chefs, Head Cooks, and Food Preparation and Serving Supervisors. Occupational Outlook Handbook, 2010-2011 Edition. Retrieved on October 28, 2011 from *http://www.bls.gov/oco/cg/ocos330.pdf*.

11. Bureau of Labor Statistics. Desktop Publishers. Occupational Outlook Handbook 2010-2011 Edition. Retrieved on October 28, 2011 from *http://www.bls.gov/oco/cg/ocos276.pdf*

12. Bureau of Labor Statistics. Fashion Designers. Occupational Outlook Handbook 2010-2011 Edition. Retrieved on October 28, 2011 from *http://www.bls.gov/oco/cg/ocos291.pdf*

13. Bureau of Labor Statistics. Property, Real Estate, and Community Association Managers. Occupational Outlook Handbook 2010-2011 Edition. Retrieved on October 28, 2011 from *http://www.bls.gov/oco/cg/ocos022.pdf*

14. Bureau of Labor Statistics. "Paralegal and Legal Assistants". *Occupational Outlook Handbook*, 2010-2011 Edition. June 7, 2011, *http://www.bls.gov/oco/ocos114.htm#training*. [accessed October 28, 2011].

15. De Roos, Dolf. *Commercial Real Estate Investing: A Creative Guide to Successfully Making Money*. Hoboken, NJ. John Wiley & Sons, Inc, 2008.

16. Definitions of Physical Activity, Exercise and Fitness, *http://www.wellnessproposals.com/health-promotion/presentations/definitions-physical-activity-exercise-fitness.pdf*. [accessed on October 28, 2011]

17. Estrin, Chere B. *Paralegal Career Guide*. 2nd Ed. New York, NY. John Wiley & Sons, Inc., 1996: 5-59.

18. Frank, Scott and Heller, Andy. Buy Low, Rent Smart, Sell High: Real Estate Investing for The Long Run. Chicago, IL. Dearborn Trade Publication, 2003

19. Hoffman, Thomas. "Your help desk career: Dead end or launching pad?" *Computer World*. April 30, 2008, *http://www.computerworld.com/s/article/9080699/Your_help_desk_career_Dead_end_or_launching_pad*. [accessed October 28, 2011]

20. Lesonsky, Rieva. Start Your Own Business 4th Ed. Entrepreneur Media, Inc. 2007. Canada.

21. National Association of Legal Assistants. 2008, *http://www.nala. org/apc.aspx.* [accessed October 28, 2011].

22. National Federation of Paralegal Association (NFPA). *Model Code of Ethics and Responsibility,* 2006, *http://www.paralegals. org/associations/2270/files/Model_Code_of_Ethics_09_06.pdf.* [accessed October 28, 2011]

23. National Institute for Automotive Service Excellence. 2011, *http:// www.ase.com/home.aspx.* [accessed October 28, 2011].

24. New England College *http://www.online.nec.edu*

25. Rosenberg-McKay, Dawn. Cosmetologist, Hairdressers and Related Jobs: Career Information. About.com. 2011. Retrieved on October 28, 2011 from *http://careerplanning.about.com/cs/occupations/p/ cosmetology.htm.*

26. Sharkey, Brian J. PhD and Gaskill, Steven E. PhD. *Fitness & Health. 6th Ed. Human Kinetics.* Champaign, IL, 2007.

27. Spencer, Lori. "How Can I Broadcast a Live Web Show?" *eHow.com.* 1999-2011, *http://www.ehow.com/way_5911428_ can-broadcast-live-show_.html.* [accessed October 28, 2011].

28. The Arts & Crafts Society. 1995-2011. Retrieved on October 28, 2011 from *http://www.arts-crafts.com/archive/curorgs.shtml.*

29. University of Berkeley. (*http://groups.haas.berkeley.edu/realestate/ PhD/phdinfo.html*)

30. Waehner, Paige, About.com Guide. Calisthenics. August 18, 2008, *http://exercise.about.com/od/exerciseworkouts/g/calisthenics.htm.* [accessed October 28, 29011].

31. Weighill, Keith. Motorcycle Maintenance Techbook. Haynes Publishing 2004. Sparksford, Yeovil, Somerset, England.